Women in Northern Ireland

**University Press of Florida**

Gainesville · Tallahassee · Tampa · Boca Raton · Pensacola · Orlando · Miami · Jacksonville

Cultural

Studies and

Material

Conditions

Megan Sullivan

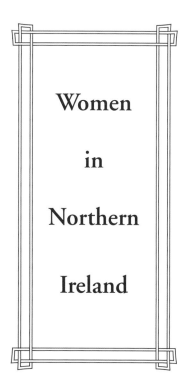

Women

in

Northern

Ireland

04  03  02  01  00  99  6  5  4  3  2  1

LIBRARY OF CONGRESS CATALOGING-IN-PUBLICATION DATA
Sullivan, Megan.
Women in Northern Ireland: cultural studies
and material conditions / Megan Sullivan.
p. cm.
Includes bibliographical references and index.
ISBN 0-8130-1698-3 (cloth: alk. paper)
1. English literature—Northern Ireland—History and criticism.
2. Women and literature—Northern Ireland—History—20th
century. 3. English literature—Irish authors—History and
criticism. 4. English literature—Women authors—History and
criticism. 5. Women in the performing arts—Northern Ireland.
6. Women—Northern Ireland—Social conditions. I. Title.
PR8891.N67S75    1999
820.9'9287'09416—dc21    99-29744

The University Press of Florida is the scholarly publishing agency
for the State University System of Florida, comprised of Florida
A & M University, Florida Atlantic University, Florida Interna-
tional University, Florida State University, University of Central
Florida, University of Florida, University of North Florida,
University of South Florida, and University of West Florida.

University Press of Florida
15 Northwest 15th Street
Gainesville, FL 32611–2079
http://www.upf.com

To Marita Galvin Sullivan

# CONTENTS

*Women in Northern Ireland: Cultural Studies and Material Conditions* develops a method of reading women in Northern Ireland by examining their fiction, nonfiction, film, and theater through the lens of Irish cultural studies. The work draws on history, literature, cinema, economics, law, drama, and women's studies. The readership I address includes practitioners of Irish studies, women's studies, literature, film, political science, and cultural studies. The text can be of benefit to advanced undergraduates, graduate students, and scholars as well as the general public in the United States, the Republic and Northern Ireland, the United Kingdom, and elsewhere. Ultimately, I wish to emphasize the richly textured lives of women in Northern Ireland and to explore the possibilities for their future, as well as for the future of Irish cultural studies.

In an attempt to acknowledge the political ideologies of many people, I use the terms "the Republic of Ireland" and "Northern Ireland" whenever possible. When referring to the words, research, or data of another, I use that person's terminology when speaking about his/her research and incorporate the designations the Republic and Northern Ireland in my analysis or commentary. For ease, footnotes have been incorporated into the text, but I can provide more extensive footnote information.

For their insightful readings of early drafts of this book, I wish to thank Mary Cappello, Jean Walton, Richard Neuse, Cheryl Foster, and Walter Sillapoa, all of the University of Rhode Island. I would also like to thank William T. O'Malley and the University of Rhode Island library. I am grateful to the reviewers of my manuscript, particularly Anne Owen Weekes. Most especially, I would like to thank Susan Fernandez at the University Press of Florida.

# Cultural Studies

# and Material

# Conditions:

# (Some) Women in

# Northern Ireland

This book argues that although debates about Northern Ireland are usually framed around political identities—Irish, British, Northern Irish; nationalist, Unionist, dissenter; Protestant and Catholic—fiction and nonfiction as well as film and theater by women make it clear that for them, broadly conceived political allegiances often obscure material conditions. While nationalist women in particular recognize the difficulties caused by the troubles and colonization, they often refuse to name either force as the only or even the largest factor in their lives. Contemporary writing and film by and about women in the North reflect this. Fiction by Mary Beckett (1987); film by Pat Murphy (1981, codirected with John Davis; 1984), Margo Harkin (1988), Orla Walsh (1992), and Anne Crilly (1988); drama by Charabanc Theatre Company (1983, 1985, 1987); and prison narratives by Margaretta D'Arcy (1981), the Gillespie sisters (1987), Gerry Adams (1990),

Brian Campbell et al. (1994), Roisin McAliskey (1998), and female Republican prisoners (1992, POW's Maghaberry) compel us to examine women's material conditions. In their fiction, film, nonfiction, and theater, women urge us to recognize the problems that result from poverty, unemployment, inadequate housing, violence and domestic abuse, sexuality, and incarceration.

I became convinced of the primacy of women's attention to material conditions when I lived in the Republic of Ireland and researched part of this book. In 1994 I met with scores of women and participated in many conferences convened by them. In a two-part conference funded by the British Council's Co-operation North and held in Dublin and Belfast, I listened as Protestant, Catholic, Jewish, and agnostic women talked about their hope for future peace in Northern Ireland. Yet, ultimately, the women spent most of the time discussing crèche facilities, employment opportunities, integrated education, voter registration, "male politicians," grief, violence, and domestic abuse. Though they spoke about the need for an end to the conflict in Northern Ireland, the women focused on material conditions, not political ideology. Interestingly, however, although they recognized the importance of economic and cultural conditions in and for their lives, and while they could respectfully agree to disagree on substantial issues such as integrated education, the women could not come to terms with incarceration. Although the subject was discussed, incarceration was the only issue for which the women did not make a postconference follow-up plan.

As I continued my research, I began to see the subject of imprisonment surface in fiction and film about nationalist women. What became apparent was that the trope of incarceration stood as a figurative example of women's imprisonment by patriarchal forces, whether those forces were nationalist, Republican, or British. Incarceration also served as a literal representation of the material needs of women who were themselves imprisoned or who had spent years visiting male relatives in jail. The mise-en-scène of the prison revealed the complex position of nationalist and Republican women whose needs remained unacknowledged by state and colonial powers as well as within the very movements in which they participated.

In order to delineate women's attention to material conditions and to suggest the possibilities for what I am terming an "Irish cultural studies," I first provide examples of how women shift the focus from what are considered broad-based political concerns to material conditions. Next, I examine how we can create and utilize a specifically Irish cultural studies.

## Material Conditions

In various texts, many women in Northern Ireland note that while they are in *partial* agreement with the male leaders who are negotiating Ireland's future, they have additional concerns. For example, although they too stress the need for a cessation of violence on all sides—including on the side of the state—women call for an examination not only of the context that has allowed violence but also of the specific effects of violence upon women. Women have been particularly eloquent in their theorizations of the gendered nature of violence in Northern Ireland, or, rather, of the troubling intersections of sexism, sectarianism, and state intervention. Recalling the misogyny demonstrated with the murders of two women, feminists have claimed that sexism and male violence will not necessarily cease after the conflict has been resolved because violence against women is not explored in broader discussions of peace.

In the 1990s, the murders of Margaret Wright and Anne Marie Smyth received particular attention in a region where many killings are noted as merely an increase in the sectarian body count. In the spring of 1994, Margaret Wright was killed in a loyalist drinking den in Belfast. Paramilitaries later disclosed that they had mistakenly assumed the woman was a Catholic. Protestant organizations decried the incident, and loyalist paramilitaries were said to have conducted an "internal investigation" of the event. In response, they shot a man thought to have murdered Wright and destroyed the den. Many were outraged at what they took to be an indication that the paramilitaries were sorry they "got" the wrong woman, not that a woman had been killed. Also, it appeared that they would not have regretted killing a Catholic. Wright's murder is often juxtaposed to Smyth's. Anne Marie Smyth was killed in 1993 and was targeted because she was a Catholic. Feminists have argued that both women were killed by men who wanted to kill females; they note the specifically gendered nature of the murders: Wright was found naked, and loyalists supposed that they acted in a chivalrous manner when they closed the den and killed the murderer, presumably out of respect for an erroneously slain female. Women insist that these murders demonstrate how sectarianism fosters sexism. Feminists recognize, too, the role misogyny plays in sectarian crimes (McWilliams 1994b, 24–25).

In 1995, Irish feminist and critic Monica McWilliams succinctly stated the issue in "Struggling for Peace and Justice: Reflections on Women's Activism in Northern Ireland": "Since the ceasefire declaration of August and October, much discussion has taken place over the decommissioning of paramilitary weapons and the demilitarization of the security forces. The use of these military weapons in situations of domestic violence has not, however, been central to these discussions" (15). Elsewhere McWilliams cogently argues that domestic violence and sexist sectarianism should be read for the ways they are encouraged by constructions of masculinity (rather than as instances of individual deviance), and she indicates that in Northern Ireland there is a peculiar problematic: the militaristic nature of the state means that weapons have been more available than in other sites, and that these weapons have often been used against women. Although not many people have tried to calculate the membership of Republican and Unionist paramilitaries, some maintain that the number surely reaches into the thousands. It has been estimated, however, that there are currently twenty thousand members in the security forces; these forces are largely composed of males who have access to weapons. Therefore, McWilliams argues that central to any peace settlement must be a reconsideration of the relationships between men and women, relationships informed by sectarianism and sexism (1994b, 24).

Some insist that the problem of violence against women is difficult to confront because women themselves are often placed in a precarious position vis-a-vis men and political struggle, a position which indicates the specific difficulties women may encounter after resolution of the conflict. If they currently find it difficult to vocalize their inequality because they are encouraged to support the "broader" political struggle and not to "detract" from the main issues, will women be encouraged not to speak after the conflict has been resolved for fear that they will shed a "bad light" on those who are working toward a different Northern Ireland? Feminists have correctly begun to argue that while women do feel alienated from the broader political struggle, they also have a complex relationship with the movement that should be able to assist them: the women's movement.

One example of controversy within the women's movement concerns the relatively well attended conference held in Belfast on March 12, 1994. Members of the Northern Irish women's group Clar Siochana na mBan convened "Women's Agenda for Peace." The conference was applauded for its elaboration of women's difficult position but was itself censured for its exclusion of Protestant women (Hackett and Quiery). The controversy highlights two issues. First, there is a need for greater collaboration among nationalist, Protestant, and unaffiliated women. Although this collaboration does occur on some levels, it does not permeate all feminist discussions. Second, as two participants in the conference note, the controversy can remind us of the questions nationalist women often ask: Should women organize around their own agenda to protect their rights and achieve true equality in society? Or should they throw their shoulders to the wheel of the struggle for national self-determination (Hackett and Quiery, 16)?

Touché for women's struggle against violence and other forms of oppression. The question is do women speak out against the men who are themselves fighting for equality, or do they suffer silently? How does the women's movement support women's struggle regardless of political differences, and thus include Protestant and other women who have heretofore felt alienated from a movement where some are sympathetic to nationalism? If the movement becomes more accessible to all women, will political differences be tolerated?

Feminists in the Republic and Northern Ireland have covered this terrain before. Many women have not participated in the women's movement in the Republic of Ireland because they could not understand women who insisted that their struggle for national unity superseded their fight for gender equality. Similarly, while some in England have supported Irish women, their support has often been either uncritical of Britain's responsibility in the North or, alternately, critical but ill informed. However, although feminists in Northern Ireland recognize these obstacles, they are hopeful that the negotiations women in the North have made and have encouraged others to make can eventually benefit women's movements worldwide.

Those who believe that feminists can learn from the struggles in Ireland note that in Northern Ireland the women's movement has been strongest and most appropriately united when it has addressed material conditions. When they provide information booklets on health concerns, welfare benefits, and other "cross-cultural/political" issues, women as a group are most successful. The success of the movement is evident when women work together to provide child-care facilities, lead antipoverty campaigns, protest inadequate housing, and interact with women in the trade union to address their employment inequality (McWilams 1991, 91–94).

Avila Kilmurray traces what she sees as the process of feminist and class activism in the North. She notes that although by the mid-1970s the working classes were silenced and female working-class issues denied altogether, by the late 1970s and 1980s, "women from the communities" did respond to what they had formerly viewed as "middle-class" feminism. According to Kilmurray, it is only recently that this response has become more prominent as women in the trade union have joined community workers and feminists to question what they view as middle-class feminism.

She suggests that the difficulties and the possibilities afforded when the women's movement, trade unionists, community workers, and grassroots political activists cooperate are demonstrated by what has become known as the annual Women's Information Day. Begun by women and community workers in Belfast in 1980, Women's Information Day seeks to bring females together under the supposition that knowledge via practical information is power. Kilmurray states that although there are many women whose political allegiances would disallow their participation in the day, the event's extraordinary power is exemplified by the fact that it continued despite the divisive marches during the hunger strikes (1981) and the fervor surrounding the Anglo-Irish Agreement (1985). The day aims to provide information on everything from health care, to crèche facilities, to welfare benefits, to community groups. Kilmurray's description of the difficulty and possibility exemplified by the day is worth quoting in full here:

the women continued to meet together [during the hunger strikes and the Anglo-Irish Agreement] because they were discussing "women's issues"—such as health, child-care, rent increases, social security cuts and the like—the type of concerns only grudgingly admitted as political in the constitutional ferment of Northern Ireland. Within the Day's set conversation/information pieces, Orange and Green divisiveness is carefully filtered out, although the harsh realities of living in Belfast intrude—the inevitable one-to-one conversations of a son kneecapped, a brother imprisoned or a father in the Ulster Defense Regiment, alongside a toddler with teething problems or a child playing truant from school. (182–83)

Kilmurray argues that Women's Information Day is a day that exemplifies the possibilities of a united working-class women's movement (183). Women can unite to find solutions to economic and cultural inequality. At the same time, the women can respect each other's political differences.

The extraordinary possibilities that could be afforded by a more stable, class-conscious women's movement, and the hope many have placed within this movement, are evident in the words of a participant in the "Women's Agenda for Peace Conference": "It is up to the women's movement to build an undeniable force, to maintain the pressure that will ensure that when the politicians talk of peace, they mean peace with justice and when they talk about guarantees, they mean a guarantee of equality for all citizens of this country" (quoted in McWilliams 1995, 32). Because so many have confidence in the women's movement in Northern Ireland, because women's strength and commitment have made change possible there, and because this movement has much to teach all, it can be a powerful force and can work toward the goal of full equality for women.

However, people in the women's movement cannot agree on the significance of incarceration. Although throughout the colonial struggle between Ireland and Britain internment and imprisonment have been complex issues, in the 1980s tensions related to incarceration revealed the schisms within the women's movement and among women more generally. According to Eileen Evanson in *Against the Grain: The Contemporary Women's Movement in Northern Ireland*, there have always been tensions simmering within the women's movement, but when women in Armagh Prison went on strike, these differences were brought to a head (19). Additionally, in "Women on the Margin: The Women's Movement in Northern Ireland, 1973–1988," Carmel Roulston argues that while some of the problems within the Northern Irish movement were comparable to tensions in other modern feminist coalitions, the issue that dissolved one of the most long-standing collectives was the campaign for political status waged by Republican prisoners. Finally, in "Political Division, Practical Alliance: Problems for Women in Conflict," Eilish Rooney notes that "at crisis points in the political conflict feminists from both sides have been forced to take up a political position. These crises have frequently centered on prison protests" (1995a, 44).

When the Republican prisoners in Armagh Prison went on a "no-wash" strike to support male prisoners and to gain political status, they smeared excrement and menstrual blood in their cells. The women were making it clear that they were intimately involved with the "bloodshed" of war and the "dirty business" of politics. Some feminists wanted to support the prisoners as women on the issue of bodily integrity, but others could not support females who were Republicans. Disagreement over the Armagh strike in particular, and the situation of Republican prisoners more generally, seriously destabilized the women's movement in the North.

The specter of the prison and women's disagreement about it remain significant in the 1990s. As previously noted, at the end of the conference I attended in Dublin and Belfast, the other participants and I listed the issues that we had discussed and made action plans for the future of Northern Ireland. Because there were diverse political and class divides represented at the conference, women could not agree to include an examination of incarceration in their vision for a future Northern Ireland. This was especially interesting because some participants had been directly affected by imprisonment and others obviously had residual feelings about prisoners. However, in light of the number of people who have been incarcerated in Northern Ireland, and because political protest and criminality are frequently discussed and reported in the region, we must examine incarceration.

The site and trope of the prison are evident when we study culture in Northern Ireland, but we need particular methods to suggest the relations among gender, incarceration, class, the state, and other material conditions.

## Irish Cultural Studies

While some practitioners of cultural studies indicate the significance of "relationality" in and for their work, others correctly insist that location is paramount. Scholars who write about Ireland are particularly attuned to the specific needs of what I am terming here "Irish cultural studies," a methodology that can and should be specific to Ireland, but which also plays out—albeit differently—in other locations. In *Anomalous States: Irish Writing and the Post-Colonial Moment*, David Lloyd argues that any radical cultural studies in Ireland must engage with an analysis of class and a critique of the state, and in "Neglecting the Material Dimension: Irish Intellectuals and the Problem of Identity," Liam O'Dowd maintains that, problematically, what he terms the "new cultural studies" in Ireland has sought to provide a more complex reading of identity rather than investigate "how changing material circumstances have shaped conceptions of identity and, by extension, the role of intellectuals" (1989, 8). O'Dowd urges an analysis of Ireland that considers economic, class, and power relations; like Lloyd, O'Dowd suggests an examination of the state as a starting point for an exploration of class and material conditions. Yet to focus upon the state alone is to neglect women's particular needs as revealed by their relation to this entity. Also, when we focus on the state, we assume it is the primary problem rather than merely one force that oppresses women. Instead, the focus should be on the state and its effect on/as *a* material condition.

To understand material relations and conditions, one must examine the quintessential theory of materialism as outlined by Karl Marx and Friedrich Engels in *The German Ideology*. In that work Marx and Engels recognize men [*sic*] as producers and products of history. All history is bound up with industry, the economy, and economic conditions (18). Thus they define material conditions as those historical/economic/material forces that create individuals (7). The individual is constructed in response to and as a result of how she lives, acts, and produces (that is, history, commodities). Because women are inadequately theorized by Marx and Engels, feminists such as Juliet Mitchell, Michele Barret, Kate Mitchell, Angela Davis, Christine Delphy, Monique Wittig, and others have long expanded this definition of material conditions. More recently, women have elaborated a theory that focuses on the materialism of Marx and Engels but foregrounds gender. They have called this materialist-feminism (Newton and Rosenfelt). Demonstrating both the radical possibility inherent in an emphasis on gender and economic considerations, and acknowledging the vexed relations among worldwide feminisms and feminist theories, still others urge a reevaluation of the terms of materialist-feminism. Their reading of literary and popular texts foregrounds the role of imperialism and the global economy in our reading strategies and in the construction of texts; those who question materialist-feminism also begin to reintroduce the importance of the state to a reading of (post)coloniality, while nevertheless foregrounding gender (Hennessey and Mohan). These extensions merely reinforce the importance of the state for Irish cultural studies and materialism but do so by suggesting that the state alone is often not the problem. Although some have argued that *because* violent confrontations have been a recurring feature of Northern Ireland the key to understanding the conflict is to examine the state (Ackroyd, 45), feminists encourage us to extend this analysis.

In any case, an analysis of the state in Northern Ireland can be a complex venture, not least of all because there is more than one state concerned. Although most scholars take the British military and Northern Irish police force (Royal Ulster Constabulary, or RUC) as principal state apparatuses, obviously the state is and participates in far more than its military operations. Additionally, in the contemporary texts of Northern Irish women, the military and police apparatuses certainly figure, but it is the oppression and resistance connected with another state and colonial institution that is more fully suggested. The prison is the state and colonial apparatus where women's relation to Republicanism, nationalism, and material conditions is underscored.

Scholars have estimated that over the last seventeen years, at least one hundred thousand people have been directly affected by imprisonment in the North (Coulter 1991, 12). Also, more than one scholar has noted that Northern Ireland is anomalous to the extent that it has the highest rate in the United Kingdom of prisoners receiving a life sentence and one of the highest percentage rates of life convictions in the world, making it a specific site for review of human rights violations and legal status evaluations. Perhaps for these reasons alone, a prison experience manifests itself in the texts I analyze. Yet one's reading of material conditions should encompass the site of the prison for other reasons as well. Because the Irish Republican Army (IRA) has often waged its anticolonial struggle in the United Kingdom and Northern Ireland, and because loyalist forces have sometimes targeted the Republic as well as the North, Northern Ireland's prison population is scattered throughout all three regions and debunks the myth that one's prison status affects only or primarily one's nation. Northern Ireland's prison population becomes Britain and the Republic and Northern Ireland's "problem," thus confounding (bourgeois) definitions of individual punishment, crime, and responsibility.

The prison is a significant indicator of the material conditions inflicted by state and (post)colonial forces because in Northern Ireland, the prison and incarceration have been subject to both state and colonial control. Indeed, one example might be that the British government mandated the Special Powers Act that made internment legal and the Northern Irish police force actually interned people; thus British (colonial) and Northern Ireland (state) forces work in consort to imprison people. In what has become known as the "IRA Roundup" of 1972, British soldiers made a list of those to be interned, while members of the RUC actually took those listed out of their homes. Also, because currently the fate of Northern Ireland's political prisoners is at issue for Republicans and others participating in the peace process, and because the release of prisoners figures prominently in debates regarding conflict resolution, the site of the prison is one of the oppressive state forces upon which I have chosen to concentrate my analysis (Cullen).

Certainly, however, the state and the prison cannot be discussed without foregrounding class, because economic conditions are made manifest by prisoners and by those who argue for a more democratic Northern Ireland. In the texts I read, where the prison is often that site which makes clear how women's needs are elided by nationalists, Republicans, and state and colonial control, it is by naming themselves as workers and/or invoking class concerns that women suggest a different future for the North.

In his exploration of what he views as one of the most repressive of all institutions, Foucault examines the prison; significantly, he analyses the European, though not necessarily the (post)colonial, jail. He notes not only the eventual progression from public execution and torture within the penal system but also the growing distance from the body as a physical site of punishment. The former physical punishment by torture and execution has given away to surveillance and disavowal performed by/engaged in by wardens, doctors, chaplains, psychiatrists, and others. According to Foucault, "The body now serves as an instrument or intermediary: if one intervenes upon it to imprison it, *or to make it work,* it is in order to deprive the individual of a liberty that is regarded both as a right and as property" (1977, 11; emphasis mine). This move away from the public sphere of physical punishment and toward more localized surveillance and domination not only marks authority's move toward a disciplining of the body politic but also indicates the power-knowledge relations in state institutions such as the prison.

Significantly, it is often overlooked that in his study of the birth of the prison, Foucault connects the prisoner and the worker. He equates imprisoning a body with forcing it to work; both are material conditions, and in both one person or institution extracts something from another. Foucault's conflation of the worker and the prisoner subtly informs my project. Yet if it is the materiality (Foucault's word) of the soul and body that interests him, what happens when we read the female body (and soul) as a worker? What happens when a woman defines herself as a worker to subvert nationalism or Republicanism as well as state and colonial powers?

Because each of the chapters in this book argues for a more complex elaboration of gender and material conditions as suggested by the site and trope of the prison, they necessarily wrestle with contemporary critical theory. I begin chapter 1, "Roisin McAliskey and the Discourse of Incarceration: Gendered Prison Narratives," by examining the rhetoric of the 1996 arrest of McAliskey. Her case demonstrates a female political prisoner's complex needs and daily realities and asks us to query what will become of her after the conflict in Northern Ireland is resolved. In an open letter that she wrote from prison, McAliskey urges an examination of the penal system. After I discuss McAliskey, I analyze prison narratives by women and men to suggest that whereas those by the nationalist and Republican women call for attention to specific concerns inside and outside the prison, the male narratives describe male camaraderie and victimization and, as such, offer less concrete proposals for the future. The prison narratives I examine are Aine and Eibhlin Nic Giolla (Easpaig) Gillespie's *Sisters in Cells: Two Republican Prisoners in England* (1987), Margaretta D'Arcy's *Tell Them Everything: A Sojourn in the Prison of Her Majesty Queen Elizabeth at Ard Macha (Armagh)* (1981), *Women in Struggle? Mina I Streachailt* issued by Sinn Fein's Women's Department (POWs Maghaberry 1992), Gerry Adams's *Cage Eleven* (1990), and *Nor Meekly Serve My Time: The H Block Struggle, 1976–1981* by Brian Campbell and others (1994).

In chapter 2, "Nationalist Ideology and Materialist Politics: Mary Beckett's *Give Them Stones*," I argue that in *Give Them Stones* (1987) Beckett's protagonist, Martha Murtagh, examines gender and nationalism. By acknowledging that her father's incarceration propels Murtagh into the workforce, Beckett's text allows for a reevaluation of the very terms the narrative invokes: Marx's "value" and "use-value." Although this chapter encourages a reconsideration of how we read all texts, the specific emphasis on the protagonist's disavowal of nationalism and recognition of gender and material conditions encourages us to more fully examine women and Marxism within (post)colonial sites. Ultimately, we are to understand that if Beckett's text reevaluates Marx's "value" and "use-value," the concept of (re)production must also be reconsidered.

In chapters 3 and 4 my reading of Irish cinema is dependent upon but also must critique dominant feminist film theory, especially as this theory is articulated in Britain and the United States. In "*Maeve* and *Anne Devlin*: Nationalism, Incarceration, and Feminist Film in Northern Ireland," I map the significance of the prison and other material conditions to theories of reading film, particularly Pat Murphy's *Maeve* (1981, codirected with John Davis) and *Anne Devlin* (1984). I also underscore the significance of writing, particularly when writing emerges in and as a result of the prison. Finally, I question how Irish history can be rewritten to include the class consciousness of women. In "Feminist Film after Pat Murphy: *Mother Ireland, Hush-A-Bye Baby,* and *The Visit,*" I analyze Anne Crilly's *Mother Ireland* (1988), Margo Harkin's *Hush-*

*A-Bye Baby* (1989), and Orla Walsh's *The Visit* (1992) to demonstrate how film theory articulated in London in the 1980s excluded the Republic and Northern Ireland and therefore calls into question hegemonic feminist theory. The chapter analyzes the aforementioned cinema for signs of cultural crisises/turning points in the Republic and Northern Ireland such as the divorce and abortion referenda, censorship, and women's sexuality. I also examine what is perhaps a subtle preoccupation throughout my project: the women's movement.

By providing theatergoers and readers with characters who represent less individual subjects and more the cultural impact of economic and gender inequality, Charabanc Theatre Company calls attention to the material needs and daily problems of women in Northern Ireland. In chapter 5, "'Politics, That's the Nub of It': Charabanc Theatre Company and the (Collective) Economy of Production," I argue that Northern Ireland's most famous female theater group draws attention not to nationalism, Republicanism, or Unionism exclusively, but rather to the political economy through women's relationship to labor, the police and paramilitary forces, legal strictures, sexuality, and domestic abuse in Ireland. When I read *Lay Up Your Ends* (1983), *Now You're Talkin'* (1985), and *Somewhere over the Balcony* (1987), I also have in mind Gayatri Spivak's emphasis on "subject formations"; specifically with regard to (post)colonial women, Spivak encourages us to examine the distinction between reifying a subject and locating and analyzing how the subject is formed through the state and political economy. Charabanc Theatre Company officially closed its doors in 1995, but I speak about the company in the present tense because its plays remain a powerful and important part of women's art and critique in Northern Ireland.

Finally, in my conclusion I examine the institutions and conditions some women think might be helpful to them in a future Northern Ireland. Certainly, I mean the conclusion to suggest as well how Irish cultural studies can continue to read texts. In fact, the texts I have chosen to examine throughout this book represent both traditionally sanctioned genres within Irish studies—fiction, theater, and, to a lesser extent, film—and those texts that provide an opportunity for a more richly conceived Irish cultural studies— prison narratives, censorship, and the women's movement, for example. Ultimately, this book is an acknowledgment of what women's responses to colonial, state, and patriarchal conflict in Northern Ireland have to teach me and other women and men about women in Northern Ireland, material conditions, and Irish cultural studies.

Roisin McAliskey

and the Discourse

of Incarceration:

Gendered Prison

Narratives

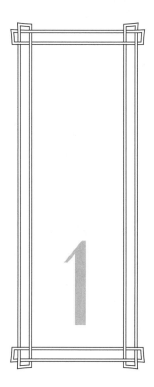

1

IN MARCH OF 1998, British home secretary Jack Straw freed Roisin McAliskey, twenty-six-year-old daughter of Bernadette Devlin McAliskey, civil rights activist and former MP for Mid-Ulster (1969–74). In 1996, Roisin was taken from her mother's home in County Tyrone, Northern Ireland, and interrogated at Castlereagh Detention Center for six days. Though she was never officially charged, McAliskey was incarcerated in connection with an IRA attack on a British army barrack in Germany. When Straw freed her, he did so by quoting psychiatric reports that said extraditing McAliskey to Germany would be "unjust and oppressive." Besides, it was doubtful that the evidence used to imprison her would be upheld in court. One man who had originally identified McAliskey as the perpetrator later recanted; handwriting analyses used against her were never corroborated; the fingerprints found at the scene could have been placed there (Britain and Ireland Human Rights Centre 1997). Besides, according to Devlin McAliskey (1997), McAliskey was working in Northern Ireland at the time of the mortar attack. For the purposes of this book, the details surrounding McAliskey are most important because they demonstrate how her case has been gendered. In the details we find how others have perceived her story and what McAliskey's case tells us about women and material conditions.

Prison narratives and the way the public perceives imprisonment testify to the material conditions that beset women in the North. Ultimately, when we analyze narratives of incarceration by Northern Irish prisoners, we see that texts by women suggest clear plans of action and outline the relation between their stories and the material, social, and economic conditions for women inside and outside prison. In contradistinction, male narratives of incarceration tend to focus on particular scenes of British injustice and on the relationship between male inmates. Let us begin our exploration of prison narratives by examining cases such as McAliskey's to discern how she was constructed and then move toward narratives written by other prisoners.

McAliskey was viewed as a pregnant female because she was pregnant at the time of her arrest; some suggest that the British government used her pregnancy to intimidate her. When the government of the Republic discussed McAliskey's case, it usually spoke first of her pregnancy, highlighting her gender. Though her family seemed most concerned with McAliskey's overall health and treatment in prison, it too discussed her pregnancy. Yet, ultimately, McAliskey and her family asked that McAliskey's case be seen as an example of an oppressive state.

Though she had never been arrested before, and despite the fact that nobody was hurt in the mortar attack she was accused of participating in, McAliskey was automatically categorized as Special Category A Prisoner; this categorization created particular problems for her as a woman and was decried by an international community. McAliskey was regularly strip-searched, had limited access to visitors, and had restricted exercise. While these conditions would have been difficult for any prisoner, they were especially counterproductive for a pregnant woman: McAliskey's body was changing, and regular strip-searching made her more uncomfortable; the limited exercise could have hurt the fetus. Moreover, McAliskey has said she was told that prison authorities planned for her to give birth shackled to guards, and that her child could be taken away from her after birth; with limited access to visitors, she found it hard not to believe this story. McAliskey's security status meant that she had two guards with her at all times and that she was not allowed to use the mother and infant birthing center at Holloway (Britain's women's prison) if others were there at the same time. Most likely there would be other women using the center when McAliskey was to give birth. The point here is that while Special Category A status is no doubt difficult for all prisoners, it is especially confining for pregnant women.

Eventually, McAliskey's security status was downgraded to Category A; while she was still guarded and under heavy restrictions, she was allowed to be hospitalized for the birth of her child. She gave birth in a London psychiatric hospital, where she remained until she was said to be well enough to return to Northern Ireland. That McAliskey's incarceration would be gendered, however, was obvious immediately after she was taken into custody.

McAliskey's interrogation after her arrest suggests that police treated her in a particular way because she was a woman and because she was the daughter of a political activist. According to independent reports by human rights organizations, after she was arrested, McAliskey was interrogated for six days and for twelve hours per day. In an attempt to psychologically damage her and to demonstrate that they saw McAliskey as a product of a Republican family, at one point during the interrogation the police brought in an officer who fifteen years earlier had carried McAliskey's sister and brother outside the home where their parents lay critically wounded by loyalist gunfire. Roisin was unharmed during the shooting. The officer recounted the events of the day her parents were shot. After interrogation and because of her security status, McAliskey was flown to an all-male prison in London. She was placed in a cell within a cell of seventy males; the cell was dirty and was said to have been used by men on the dirt strike (Britain and Ireland Human Rights Centre). Although this could be seen as a way Roisin McAliskey was desexed, putting her in a male cell actually had the effect of highlighting not only that she was a woman but also that she was an extraordinarily deviant woman. Why else would she need to be placed in a male cell, a cell formerly occupied by the most intransigent prisoners? But it was not this "desexing" that proved most harmful. According to several reports, when she was brought to London, the police psychiatrist said that her initial interrogation had already damaged McAliskey's mental health.

McAliskey's gender also had a direct effect on the economics of her incarceration. When she was three days away from going into labor, the British government allowed that McAliskey could be transferred to a hospital to give birth. According to her solicitor, Gareth Peirce, and as reported in several newspapers, there were strict rules regarding the transfer: McAliskey must agree to reside twenty-four hours per day in the hospital's mother and baby unit; her family must pay a surety of £100,000; a £95,000 security note must be deposited with her solicitors; and she must agree to consent to all future medical and psychiatric reports. A pregnant, incarcerated women categorized as a high risk must pay money to the government if she wants to deliver her baby in a hospital.

There was an international outcry against McAliskey's arrest, an outcry which often focused on her treatment as a pregnant woman. A House of Commons motion echoed Amnesty International's contention that "if she is still in custody at the time of her confinement, she will not be able to use the mother and baby unit at Holloway Prison if it is being used by other prisoners" (Borrill). The British government was urged to reconsider its "cruel, inhumane and degrading treatment" of the prisoner (Borrill). The Republic of Ireland had not pushed for bail for McAliskey because it understood that "Miss McAliskey could not be involved in any subversive action while heavily pregnant or in labor" (Ford). The Republic's response to McAliskey is interesting on two levels: One, the government was working hard to broker a peace settlement and would want to be seen as supportive of the daughter of a nationalist activist. Second, enshrined in the government's constitution is a recognition of a woman's special role as a mother. When it made the case that McAliskey could not be involved in terrorist activity because she was pregnant and therefore did not need bail to be moved to a hospital, the government in the Republic was relying on preconceived notions of motherhood. To be a mother means not to be a terrorist. While I have no desire to argue the feasibility of being a mother and a terrorist, I do want to suggest that from the beginning, McAliskey was perceived as a mother by both governments. The discourse of these responses underscores the specifically gendered nature of McAliskey's case, yet the support for McAliskey is more helpful when it moves from the personal to a discussion of women's particular material concerns with respect to incarceration.

As a result of McAliskey's imprisonment, the European Parliament, in its annual human rights report, called for "provisions throughout the EU of appropriate facilities for pregnant women held in detention" (O'Sullivan). In the same report, Ireland was criticized for its "restriction of freedom of opinion where a law prohibits publication of any material in favor of abortion" (O'Sullivan). Thus, in one report, the connection was made between women's position in Irish society—their right to information regarding reproductive choice—and the inadequate facilities for Irish women in British prisons. The lack of provisions for women within Irish culture is reflected in British and Irish prisons, where women are not guaranteed particular freedoms and are punished in a way that is perceived to be most harmful to them as women (see chapter 3 for a fuller explanation of the effects of gender on incarceration and punishment).

McAliskey's case is significant as well because discussion about it highlights the tension between right-to-life supporters in Ireland and pro-choice activists, a tension which was especially contentious in the 1980s and is still debated in the 1990s (see Alibhe Smyth, *The Abortion Papers*). Most virulent in its attack against a woman's right to choose has been SPUC, the Society for the Protection of Unborn Children. Yet in April, responding to McAliskey's incarceration, Dr. Mary Lucy, the president of SPUC, asked the society's sister organization in England to address prison authorities regarding McAliskey. Bernadette Devlin McAliskey has been an outspoken opponent of SPUC, and SPUC has consistently sought to represent itself as an "antipolitical" organization, by which it means that it is separate from and does not intervene into the conflict in Northern Ireland. Yet as McAliskey's case illustrates, women and their material concerns (such as pregnancy) can never be entirely separate from the conflict in Northern Ireland; by association, neither can the focus on abortion in the South be entirely separate from other political realities in the Republic and Northern Ireland. Lucy notes the unusual nature of SPUC's intervention into the McAliskey case: "We are primarily a pro-life, anti-abortion society and we have nothing to do with [political] campaigns as such, but we would also have a duty, an obligation to protect Irish mothers from the effects of abortion and to protect the life of the unborn child, so it [McAliskey's case] would be within our remit to some degree" (quoted in John Connolly).

While SPUC denies that it is a "political" organization, and while Sinn Fein's policy document on a woman's right to choose is ambivalent (see chapter 2), McAliskey's case indicates that there cannot be a separation between women's material conditions and national conflict. SPUC's involvement testifies that movements about women and their concerns and "political" movements can and do inform one another.

Because she was incarcerated, McAliskey underscored the connections between the material conditions that beset women and the conflict in Northern Ireland. Yet the discourse of the case suggests the extent to which gendered presuppositions affect and can alter national and international decisions. While it is true that because they invoked her pregnancy to discuss McAliskey, politicians and others were defining her incarceration in terms of her gendered status with all that the history of Irish womanhood suggests, it is also true that McAliskey's pregnancy has forced a recognition of inadequate policy regarding women and incarceration. Roisin McAliskey and her mother have both tried to foreground the institutional concerns about women and incarceration.

In her interview with Radio Free Eireann, Devlin McAliskey (1997) said that her daughter's arrest "formed a part of a systematic pattern of aggressive harassment and intimidation of community groups in West Belfast accompanied by the arrests of young women who worked in the area, were computer literate and were vulnerable because of pregnancy or recent childbirth." Devlin McAliskey's socialist principles encourage her to recognize institutional patterns rather than individual wrongs (see chapter 4). If she is correct, police targeted women, especially women who were perceived to be vulnerable because they were pregnant or had recently given birth. According to Devlin McAliskey, police also targeted women who were computer literate. Interestingly, in a working-class area such as West Belfast, women who are employed and who have marketable skills are said to be targets for arrest.

Roisin McAliskey was granted release in March of 1998 on the grounds of her ill mental health. However, in an open letter she posted over the Internet that month to discuss the need for institutional change in prisons, McAliskey appeared thoughtful and emotionally healthy. McAliskey's case was assisted by her family's use of the Internet and the "Free Roisin McAliskey Website." Browsers were asked to inform themselves about the case and to write letters to Roisin and on her behalf. In her open letter of thanks broadcast over the Internet to her supporters, McAliskey draws attention to the specific plight of women in prison. In the letter, McAliskey names herself as a Category A Prisoner, Holloway Prison. The overt text of the letter is that she wishes to thank people for thinking about her because incarceration has taught her that the only things people cannot take from you are your thoughts. She then begins the crux of her discussion: prison conditions. "Although everyone knows what a prison is, I don't think anyone can imagine 'how' it is until they experience it." How it is, according to McAliskey, is colorless, tasteless, and lifeless. Yet for Irish female prisoners, she states, it is even worse:

It's the closed and controlled [prison] environment that leads to closed and biased minds. Out of nearly 30 women with children in prison, only two would sit in a room with me. But when I'm treated like such a danger that I'm put in a high security male prison, why wouldn't they be fearful and object to having to associate with what is presented as a threat to the little they have for themselves. There is a prison rule that prisoners cannot share, lend or give anything to other prisoners. So that while you are removed from your family and friends, you are prevented from building new relationships. But if you are an Irish prisoner in England, they segregate you—build a prison within their prison. With the men, they house them in S.S.U.—Special Secure Unit! And as they haven't got a S.S.U. for females, I get a human equivalent, with two "shadow" officers accompanying at all times, human bookends, giving me my own prison within a prison.

According to McAliskey, Irish prisoners in Britain generally feel different from the regular prison population, but female prisoners who are treated as a security risk feel even more alienated. When the British government placed her in a male prison, the implication was that McAliskey was such a deviant woman (a terrorist) that she could not be housed with "ordinary decent" female prisoners. When they treated her as a security risk because they considered her a Republican and because of her mother's political activity, the British government set the stage for McAliskey to be ostracized.

The case of Roisin McAliskey was most productively analyzed when it was discussed in terms of specific material concerns for women, especially their treatment when incarcerated. Her case should also be contextualized within what I am calling here prison narratives, or the discourse of incarceration. Taken together, male and female prison narratives will indicate how we read incarceration.

## Male Incarceration Narratives: Camaraderie and Oppression

When they acknowledge female nationalists or Republicans at all, men often construct women as long-suffering martyrs for the Irish cause; Irish men who are incarcerated describe themselves as the ones who are oppressed. However, the men also construct their heroism and their camaraderie with other Republican men. In *Cage Eleven* Gerry Adams writes about his coming of age in prison. In the foreword to his book, Adams acknowledges that his chapters, most of them derived from articles he wrote while he was incarcerated and published in Republican journals, are "light-hearted" (13). He assures the reader that Long Kesh Prison was not a happy place, but that nevertheless "POWs were happy, funny, enjoyable people who made the best of their predicament" (13). This ethos of making the best of a bad situation not only would be familiar to an Irish audience (and to those who recognize the Republic and Northern Ireland's beleaguered history) but also underscores the resiliency of Republican men.

*Cage Eleven* was published in 1990 when Adams had already been president of Sinn Fein and MP for West Belfast, so it is unclear whether or not the foreword, with its more cerebral consideration of his topic, reflects his new position or simply illustrates his maturity. Written several years after his incarceration, in the foreword Adams reminds us of the importance of personal history for political prisoners, and he notes that all the males in his family have been incarcerated: "Almost twenty years have passed since Long Kesh was opened and through the years it has been a constant element in the lives of all the members of my family. On any of these many days since then at least one of us has been in there. . . . our female family members . . . have spent almost twenty years visiting prisons" (12). Like other prison narratives, Adams's acknowledges the impact of familial incarceration on a prisoner; many incarcerated Republicans grew up in families where their parents and/or siblings were also imprisoned.

Adams's consideration of the women who visited men for twenty years may reflect the movement within Sinn Fein to highlight the roles of women; according to the Sinn Fein Women's Department, Adams has been very supportive of the department's work and its efforts to remind others of the plight of women in the Republican community. In an interview with Laura E. Lyons, Mairead Keane, who was then head of Sinn Fein Women's Department, said that "Gerry Adams actively campaigns in rural and in urban areas—wherever he goes—to make sure that women are on the platform. He talks about the need to involve women in the struggle, and in Sinn Fein's Belfast office, there have been many events and efforts to recognize women's involvement in the struggle in the last twenty-some years" (Quoted in Lyons, 267).

Importantly, Adams's foreword is one of the few male prison narratives to mention women who have spent years visiting men; thus his acknowledgment of the role of some Republican women is significant. Yet the narrative itself does not discuss women in any detail; when women are mentioned, they are named as the girl-friend or wife of a prisoner. Toward the conclusion of *Cage Eleven,* Adams consoles a friend whose wife can no longer tolerate the life of a prisoner's wife, although she loves her husband. The book's table of contents also indicates that the narrative is a guide for other Republican prisoners: There are chapter headings such as "Early Risers" (negotiating the differences between cell mates and prisoners); "Screws" (understanding the guards); "The H-Block" (acknowledging the history of political protest in prison); and "Dear John" (contending with the fact that your wife might leave you when you are in prison). This last chapter is particularly poignant, but it serves to suggest the friendship and camaraderie of two men and does not focus on the woman. In this final section, Adams describes how he consoled his fellow prisoner whose wife has just told him she wants a separation: "He didn't look at me. He didn't need to. He knew I cried with him, sad little tears of solidarity and love" (148). The two are so close, and Adams is so empathetic as a fellow Republican, that no words are needed. Adams notes, too, that he has written his story in hopes that other male and female Republican prisoners will "recognize themselves" in his words. Yet there is no chapter specific to women and their needs, nor is there a discussion of women who will wait for men to be released. Because Adams's story is told from a male perspective, one might not automatically expect to find a chapter on women, but there were women in prison when he was and when his narrative was published. However, when a female prisoner or a female family member of a prisoner reads this book, she will not find her specific plight illustrated. She will not read about the specifically gendered conditions some women writers and filmmakers explore when they discuss incarceration: economic and financial security when a partner is imprisoned; treatment of female prisoners; strip-searching and women, and women's rights in prison.

While Adams's narrative may not adequately discuss a female experience, it is important that he highlights male camaraderie. One could analyze this male friendship as merely a necessary force for the psychological survival of long-term prisoners; no doubt some would find in particular prison narratives an erotic component to male friendships as well. Yet what I find poignant here is that the male friendships described are seemingly unusual. Does this mean that some males in Northern Ireland do not readily have access to male friendships in Irish society and only find them in jail? Or is Adams subtly enticing other men into a "brother-hood" that comes with IRA membership?

Women do not necessarily focus on such female community in their narratives. Perhaps female communities are more readily available to them in Northern Ireland and are thus not the aberration in prison that they are for men. More probably, the desire for female community does not itself compel women to participate in

Republicanism. Instead, women write about what does compel them to fight: material conditions. Ultimately, though, Adams's is a male coming-of-age story, albeit one that takes place in prison. The female prison narratives I have read are not specifically coming-of-age stories because women do not focus on how they grew as women or into adulthood while imprisoned. Rather, they detail what prison reforms need to be made.

Adams provides some history of imprisonment in Northern Ireland and includes a poignant letter describing his sorrow for a family accidentally killed during an IRA mission. Yet his narrative essentially recounts the story of men who serve their time together and, in the process, form a bond. Adams and two other prisoners tell stories and laugh. One recounts his embarrassment upon being roused for an early morning prison wake-up call and finding that his pant legs had been sewn together. Of this prank played upon him by his cell mates, the prisoner states, according to Adams, "it wasn't fair, making an eeject of me in front of the Brits. Not a very Republican thing to do" (143). When he describes the pranks the men play upon one another and even when Adams recounts poignant moments of friendship and humor, he reinforces the bond between and among Republican men who are incarcerated. Yet, significantly, he never specifically suggests a call for action, nor does he use his story as an opportunity to educate others about the history of the conflict or its particular effects upon people. He also offers very little thought-provoking or intellectual discussion of incarceration.

Other narratives by men also fail to offer concrete suggestions for change, though they do suggest what is wrong with incarceration simply by detailing atrocities that take place in prison.

In accounts of the 1980 and 1981 hunger strikes and of the "H Block Struggle," male prisoners who participated in "no-wash" programs and hunger strikes describe their physical violation by prison authorities. Yet they also describe their own spirit and vitality, a vitality fostered by male camaraderie. Ultimately, male Republicans who write about incarceration construct themselves as agents of change. In *Nor Meekly Serve My Time: The H Block Struggle, 1976–1981,* Brian Campbell and his coauthors note that the blanket men (those who refused to wash and clothe in protest) were "historians, people who not only changed history but were themselves changed by it" (xvi). One prisoner describes his incarceration during the hunger strikes:

The worst thing was the constant fear. From half-seven in the morning when the screws [guards] came on to the wing until half-eight at night when they left again, we never knew the moment our door would open and two or three of them would come in to slap and punch us about. Usually it would be under the pretext of a "cell search." We all wore a blanket wrapped around our waist and at some point during the search they'd ask for a blanket as if to search it too. Then, as we stood naked, they'd invent some excuse to hit us. There's an awful feeling of defenselessness when you're standing naked in front of people who are hostile to you. (11)

While there is no doubt that men were the victims of this physical abuse, women detail physical abuse less, perhaps because they encounter the abuse less frequently, or perhaps because detailing the abuse has become a more common hallmark of the male prison narrative.

In addition to chronicling physical abuse, many prison narratives by men, especially those that discuss the 1980s, focus on the body. The Thatcher government's withdrawal of "Special Category" status in 1976 meant that Republican prisoners were not seen as political prisoners, although they were still tried and sentenced by Diplock courts. The Diplock courts replaced three-judge courts with one judge. The courts were instituted in 1972 when Lord Diplock wrote his report on possible changes to the legal system in Northern Ireland. They allowed the following: the suspension of a jury trial for certain offenses, relaxed rules on the admissibility of evidence, and wider powers of arrest for the security forces. Though the Diplock courts were set up as an attempt to find a replacement for internment, they were only slightly less barbaric than internment. When "Special Category" was withdrawn, Republican prisoners went on a "blanket protest" in 1976; they refused to wear normal prison clothes and garbed themselves in blankets. The "dirty protest" followed; the men smeared excrement on cell walls and floors. In 1980 and 1981, there were two hunger strikes. During the hunger strikes and no-wash strikes, Republican men used their bodies as sites of resistance, so their discussion of the body is understandable. Yet because of the history of Catholicism and its repression of the body, male narratives that focus on the body have a peculiar resonance in a country that has had to tolerate centuries of religious oppression and has been affected by religious indictments against the flesh.

Republican prisoners who protested by not washing themselves or their cells were sometimes physically forced to bathe. Although many narratives relate this experience as traumatic, several men suggest that even more difficult was the experience of being searched for contraband or "illicit material" such as pens and paper or cigarettes. One prisoner describes such a search: "They [the guards] would kick and punch, drag and trail us along the landing up to cell 26 where they forced us over a mirror" (Campbell et al. 88). Another prisoner recalls a similar event: "When they got me bent over the mirror one of them said he could see something. When I refused they told me to face the wall. I said 'no,' so one of them grabbed me by the hair and turned me round. Two more turned my arms upon my back. . . . then two more screws came and lifted my legs into the air. This left me upside-down with my head between my legs" (Campbell et al. 90–91). Feminists in particular have analyzed the use of one's body for political purposes; also, women have been acutely aware of how their bodies have been constructed in the public and private sphere. In the context of the Republic and Northern Ireland, and with respect to prison narratives, however, there is a difference, and that difference is colonization.

The decision of the blanket men to use their body as a form of protest had its genesis in the desire to use what had been previously brutalized: the men chose to use their bodies as sites of resistance in prison because prison guards often inflicted harm upon their bodies, and, more important, because the British government refused to see their bodies as political. Yet as some (post)colonial scholars have argued, the body of the colonized "other" is often eroticized by the colonizer. Male prisoners seek to use their body because it has been prohibited and "othered," but one wonders if when they focus on the body, Republican prison narratives necessarily subvert this eroticization. Certainly, though the above-quoted treatment of a man being searched is disquieting to a reader, it is not necessarily subversive; rather, it is descriptive. Although they refused to wear prison uniforms, prisoners did refuse to remain naked; thus, donning the blanket in the first place was an act of resistance. Republican prisoners describe their physical violation in part because they recognize that readers will be correctly appalled by this violation and will therefore be more sympathetic to their concerns, but such descriptions, *in themselves,* do not call for specific changes within the prison system. Their stories imply that change is needed. However, because they are so consumed by the intransigence of the British government, Republican men fail to locate specific agents of change elsewhere.

The no-wash protest and the hunger strikes were an attempt to force the British government to recognize not only that Republican prisoners were indeed political prisoners but also that this government must treat them as such. Social policy analyst Mike Tomlinson, with his coauthors, underscores the veracity of the inmates' contention when he states that "since the emergence of the modern prison system in the 19th century, penal policies and prison regimes in Ireland have been strongly influenced by the containment of political disorder, specifically militant Irish nationalism and republicanism" (Tomlinson, O'Dowd, and Rolston 195). Although it wishes to "criminalize" Republicans and view them as "ordinary decent criminals" who thus have no political agenda and are not fighting a political opponent, Tomlinson argues that the British government's actions with respect to incarceration suggest otherwise. Tomlinson insists that the British government clearly sees Irish prisoners as being politically motivated, and this becomes obvious when one examines the specific rules the government has constructed for the extradition, transfer, and sentencing of, and security arrangements for, Republican and loyalist prisoners.

Importantly, Tomlinson highlights the difference between the criminalization of male and female Irish political prisoners. He argues that "women political prisoners have also been subject to criminalisation, but in their case the pressure came in the form of sexual violence—the authorities' insistence in strip searching by force any prisoner who refused to comply with this 'security' measure" (219). Female prisoners have indeed written about strip searches and "sexual violence." The men in Campbell's collection do contend with sexual violence, but while the men acknowledge the abuse inflicted on their body as physical abuse, some women clearly see strip-searching as a form of sexual violence. Women perceive strip searches as a form of sexual violence because the prison instituted the policy of searches in accordance with its view of gender. Yet rather than focus on whether women and/or men see bodily abuse as sexual violence, we need to analyze how readers think about what is being done to prisoners. When they read prison narratives, scholars should be at least as attuned to audience response as are the authors of the prison narratives. Only then will they fully comprehend the significance of how women and men conceive of abuse in prison.

### Female Incarceration Narratives: Justice Now and for the Future

Two now-infamous women who were once imprisoned for alleged Republican activity have written about the rigors of prison, their political backgrounds, and the importance of the lessons of the prison for a future Ireland. These lessons encourage a recognition of women and material conditions.

On February 27, 1975, Aíne and Eibhlín Nic Giolla Easpaig (Gillespie) were sentenced to fifteen years in jail at Manchester Crown Court. They were charged with conspiracy to cause explosions because the two were found in a home where bomb explosives were being made. After they were released, they wrote about their experiences. In *Sisters in Cells: Two Republican Prisoners in England* (1987), the Gillespies begin their story by putting it in context: they describe their background and their formative years in England and Ireland. The women acknowledge that their brother's imprisonment and the fact that the Gillespie family home was searched when the two were adolescents may have influenced their political activism, though they profess to be innocent of the charges that were levied against them. Also significant is that their brother taught them Irish national history. Especially in chapter 2, this book acknowledges how the (nationalist) tutelage of young women affects them.

When they talk about the rigors of prison, the Gillespies recount strip searches: "Everything was searched before you were allowed to put any of your clothes back on—hair, ears, mouth, toes etc." (73). The problem of strip searches appears in accounts by other prisoners as well. In *Women in Struggle/Mina I Streachailt,* issued by Sinn Fein Women's Department, Republican prisoners in Maghaberry Prison (Northern Ireland's female prison) recount the 1992 forced strip-searching of Republican prisoners (POWs Maghaberry). According to one of these prisoners, after she was forcibly strip-searched and no contraband was found, guards ordered her to clothe herself. She refused. "At my insistence, they dressed me" (5). This prisoner concludes by noting that although on March 2, 1992, twenty-one Republican prisoners were forcibly strip-searched, no contraband material was found (5). She contends that the searches were "a further attempt by the jail and its administration to humiliate, degrade and control us women POWs by stripping us naked and violating our bodies in this way" (5). The prisoner states that although the event has left "my body feeling battered and abused, my mind and resolve to continue to oppose strip searches remains steadfast" (5). Importantly, in this account, the prisoner refuses not only to comply with the demands of authority but also to clothe herself—to cover up what has been done to her. Like her male counterparts, her narrative is a tale of physical violation. However, she implicitly tells us how she resists this violation by refusing to clothe herself and by forcing the authorities to cover up what they did. The female prisoner who was forcibly stripped wants the guards and the British government to see that even though they abuse her because they see her as a criminal, she will use her body as a site of political resistance. The woman who is stripped wants those who abused her to see their action not only as physical abuse but also as sexual abuse, or at least as abuse dictated by her gender. There is no similar account in the stories I read by men.

Strip searches and no-wash protests have also become important because they were obvious divisive issues within the women's movement. In the 1980s, some female prisoners embarked on a no-wash protest, and several women went on hunger strikes to protest Britain's decision to revoke political status. In her provocative article, journalist and feminist Nell McCafferty says that "It is my belief that Armagh is a feminist issue." She contends that for feminists, especially for women in the Republic and Northern Ireland who are often oppressed by religious and state doctrine, bodily integrity crosses nationalist lines. Not all in the women's movement agree, however.

In *Tell Them Everything: A Sojourn in the Prison of Her Majesty Queen Elizabeth at Ard Macha (Armagh)* (1981), the autobiographical narrative of one women's political activism and incarceration, writer Margaretta D'Arcy recalls furious debates at women's conferences in Dublin. As she remembers, when women were asked to support Republican women even if they did not agree with nationalism or Republicanism, they responded, "What about battered wives? One-parent families? Divorce? Contraception? These are the real women's issues, not trying to overthrow the state" (quoted in D'Arcy, 120). The women's movement was split between those who would support Republican women and the no-wash protest as females, and those who felt unable to support women who were convicted of Republican activity. D'Arcy states that it was "amazing how many women calling themselves feminists, closed their eyes, blocked up their ears, and ran to their political parties—Fine Gael, Sinn Fein the Workers' Party, and the Irish Labour Party—seeking urgent reassurance in the old patriarchal priorities of women's needs" (120). While I agree that the questions women asked indicated the divisions within the movement, and while chapter 2 discusses these divisions more fully, I would read the women's remarks slightly differently than does D'Arcy. The questions suggested not only women's resistance to Republicanism but also their preoccupation with their material conditions. Their questions also revealed, however, that the site of the prison brings to light these concerns. Those unable to support what they term "blowing up the state" felt this way in part because they were too concerned with their own material difficulties. Some women who could not support the female prisoners also wanted to work with the state they already had because they were not convinced that "blowing it up" would alter the status of women. Nevertheless, by calling our attention to women's responses, D'Arcy indicates what happened when the women's movement failed to acknowledge the concerns of Republican and nationalist women.

In D'Arcy's narrative of her three-month imprisonment, she describes the reaction when she and another prisoner give a lecture to other Republican prisoners and political activists. D'Arcy recounts the event: "The questions expressed what we already know to be their [Republican women's] prejudices: abortion, lesbianism, why were we [in the women's movement] men-haters, the Catholic Church" (107). The Republican prisoners, as mostly Catholic women, were fairly conservative in their beliefs and failed to see the women's movement's support of abortion and homosexuality, for example, as important to their struggle for national freedom. Their response gives credence to some in the women's movement who see the conservatism of Republican women as proof that they are subservient to Republican men, who will continue to oppress them after the conflict in Ireland has been resolved. Yet the prisoners' forceful questioning of what they viewed as the important issues within the women's movement reveals their real contention: the women's movement assumes the prisoners are handmaidens of Republican men, and fails to see the incarcerated women as autonomous agents for political change. D'Arcy underscores what she learned from her discussions with the female prisoners: "By implication we [the women's movement] were saying that the Republican Movement had not recognized their struggle in the jail as having an identity of its own and that it was no more than support for the men" (108).

The prisoners' questions, put forward during a lecture in the prison block, illustrate to D'Arcy what the women's movement had done. "We had never opened up channels of communication with them, so that they could have followed the debates, and taken the opportunity of letting their voices be heard. . . . we had been fighting on their behalf without ever asking them if they wanted it" (109). D'Arcy's narrative concludes with her solution, one she recognizes as a result of the actions of female prisoners. She notes that when three women who were serving time for alleged Republican activity went on hunger strikes for political status, they invited their "sisters in Ireland and throughout the world to stand and be counted" (quoted on 122). According to D'Arcy, their call should be understood by "women all over the world who are victims of state imperialism and personal imperialism" (122). Clearly, D'Arcy thinks international female solidarity is the answer to women's oppression. Her use of the terms "state" and "personal" imperialism suggest that she sees state oppression as equally reprehensible as "personal" imperialism. Thus, for D'Arcy, even women who do not wish to "overthrow the state" but who do feel personally oppressed (by patriarchy and economic inequality) must join forces with the female prisoners. Ultimately, in her prison narrative, D'Arcy does more than detail female friendship or bodily integrity: She advocates an international and cross-cultural female solidarity.

In the conclusion of their narrative, *Sisters in Cells: Two Republican Prisoners in England,* Aine and Eibhlin Nic Giolla Easpaig (Gillespie) suggest different solutions to the conflict in Ireland, but they also do so by centering their concerns on the site of the prison. At the end of the description of their background, arrest, and incarceration, the Gillespies announce what others must analyze in order to find a solution in Ireland. First, they speak out against the farce of prison reform: "We found in the prisons a regime ill-suited to be part of an effort by the state—by society—not only to punish prisoners but to try and reform them" (156). They think the prison system in general, and the British institution in particular, is too corrupt. They also register the hazards of inadequate prison health care, and the failure to adequately address the problems faced by Irish prisoners in Britain. They greatly lament what they see as the unproductive and degrading practice of strip-searching. They note that strip-searching has failed to provide "any apparent results that would make sense" (159).

Independent reports have confirmed their suspicions. In 1985, David Roche, chief executive officer, Irish Information Partnership, presented his report entitled *Strip Searches at Her Majesty's Prison for Women. Armagh, Northern Ireland.* According to Roche, strip searches were "reintroduced" at Armagh Prison in 1982 "in the interests of Security and the safe custody of inmates" (quoted in Roche 1) but have failed to yield appreciable results. Roche states:

> There appears to be technical doubt about the need for the practice. But there is also doubt about the technical effectiveness of mechanical substitutes. If the purpose of the strip search is to discover material such as explosives or metal objects held externally by a prisoner and which would put in jeopardy the security of the prison, metal detectors and explosive detectors are available and could be used as a substitute to some degree. Metal detectors are, for instance, used during rub-down searches in Armagh and other prisons in Northern Ireland. By the British Government's own admission, the searches do not cover the orifices and thus forbidden material (including explosives or bullets concealed in the orifices) cannot be discovered by strip searches. (8)

Roche concludes: "Therefore, on technical grounds alone, the real purpose of the strip search policy in Northern Ireland remains, in the view of the Partnership, equivocal and the necessity of the policy on security grounds is still unproven by Government statements" (8).

The report also states that the material discovered by strip searches to date "does not support the argument that the searches contribute to the maintenance of security" (8). Independent reports as well as analyses by women after their release from prison indicate the failure of strip searches. The Gillespies protest strip-searching not only because it is degrading but also because it does not work. They attack the failed logic of the activity, not the broad injustice of it.

Finally, the Gillespie sisters use their book to assert the "total innocence" of Annie Maguire, convicted with the Birmingham Eight on spurious evidence. They note, too, that when they were in prison, they were not especially friendly with Maguire. Maguire is now out of jail and still working to prove her innocence; when they assert that she is not guilty, the Gillespie sisters offer their words as a "reminder to all those in authority or with influence who have remained silent" (146). They do not focus on female friendship but rather use their prison narrative to argue for institutional change. While the sisters do not call themselves feminists and do not, as does D'Arcy, call for feminist solidarity, they do highlight the cases of other women, both those who are political prisoners and also "ordinary decent criminals."

The Gillespie sisters were released in 1983 after serving a fifteen-year jail sentence in Britain minus the legally allowable remission time, or time off for good behavior. The Armagh Jail has been closed and will be turned into a museum, as has Kilmainham Gaol, the site of the incarceration of Anne Devlin, another nationalist prisoner. New female prisons are being built in Dublin and in Northern Ireland.

Wherever they are incarcerated, female prisoners will, as we have seen, tend to write different accounts of their prison experience than will male prisoners. Female narratives call for a recognition of other female prisoners and how they demonstrate the material—economic, gender, cultural—concerns of Irish women, concerns which are brought to the forefront because women are incarcerated. Prison narratives by women also argue for institutional change inside and, by association, outside prison. Their incarceration suggests the material needs of women outside of the prison by underscoring the different forms of inequality women on the inside and outside endure because of their gender. Women writers detail injustice in many genres, but they remain consistent in their focus on specific material conditions.

In addition to prison narratives, fiction, film, and theater by women detail the complex role of nationalist and Republican women. The following chapters will examine material conditions and incarceration as written about and portrayed by women in the arts.

# Nationalist Ideology and Materialist Politics: Mary Beckett's *Give Them Stones*

"You and your United Ireland! Are you always thinking about it?" "No," I said. "I'm always thinking of baking bread and selling it and feeding my family and what they'll be when they grow up but the thought of the border's like a nail sticking up in my shoe. I've got used to it but it's never comfortable."

(Mary Beckett, *Give Them Stones*)

Of all the tools for developing alternative histories—gender, race, ethnicity, class—class is surely the most abstract. It is only when we forget this that we can set aside class-analysis as essentialist.

(Gayatri Spivak, "Who Claims Alterity")

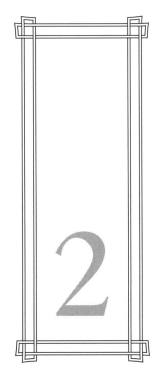

WHEN SHE ESCHEWS nationalism by labeling herself as a woman worker, Martha Murtagh, the protagonist of Mary Beckett's *Give Them Stones* (1987), complicates a nationalist narrative and foregrounds gender and material conditions in Northern Ireland. Although male writers often construct the nationalist story as one— if not *the*—dominant theme in contemporary Northern Irish fiction, Beckett provocatively insists that women are concerned with day-to-day material conditions, which are informed by the troubles, but which nevertheless cannot be reduced to them. She also reminds us of the significance of a father's imprisonment for a woman.

This chapter focuses on a female protagonist who ultimately decides to reject nationalism because it fails to adequately provide for or respond to the needs of women. While the protagonist's father's incarceration does not comprise a large part of the novel and thus will not be discussed at length here, it is an event that informs the protagonist's decision and will be recognized accordingly. While the impact of incarceration should be borne in mind throughout this chapter, it is specifically addressed in the section "Internment: Punishment, Power, and Class."

In *Give Them Stones*, Martha Murtagh is a middle-aged Catholic woman who reflects on her life in Northern Ireland. Although *Give Them Stones* sympathizes with the men who are often alternately interned or unemployed, Beckett focuses on a woman's response to the violence perpetrated by the state (Royal Ulster Constabulary, or RUC), the British government, and paramilitaries (Irish Republican Army, or IRA). The novel begins with Martha's ultimate act of resistance. When the IRA shoots a young boy in the knees in front of her shop, Martha protests by refusing to pay the protection money routinely collected by paramilitary forces, and, as a result, her home is burned. The novel is informed by Beckett's own life and history, along with the history of Northern Ireland.

# Mary Beckett and Women's Concerns
## in Northern Ireland

Mary Beckett was born in 1926 and raised in Belfast, where she attended St. Columban's National School, St. Dominic's High School, and St. Mary's Teacher Training College. She taught primary school in Catholic, working-class Ardoyne, and while there, she won a BBC radio story contest for "The Excursion." Throughout the 1950s, her stories were published in Belfast's the *Bell* and other journals and in the "New Irish Writing" section of the *Irish Press*. However, in 1956 Beckett married and moved to Dublin and discontinued writing for the next twenty years while she raised her children. Yet she remained committed to the people of Northern Ireland, and in the 1970s, frustrated by the attitudes of people in the Republic of Ireland toward the North, she began to write again.

Her first collection is aptly titled *A Belfast Woman* (1980), and these short stories indicate the themes that Beckett will examine in *Give Them Stones*. *A Belfast Woman* acknowledges and even celebrates the women who struggle daily to live in and around Belfast. While some stories focus on what might be called "domestic politics" between men and women and within families, others reveal that such "domestic" politics can never be entirely separate from national and international concerns, especially in the North.

Yet because Beckett recognizes the distinct lives of women throughout Ireland, after *Give Them Stones* she wrote *A Literary Woman* (1990), which is set in middle-class Dublin. In *A Literary Woman* a woman refuses to become engaged to a man who has kept her waiting too long; another mails letters to people and watches for signs that the lives of the recipients are crumbling; and still another takes her part in a modern marriage gone awry. Beckett's other works include children's novels, *When Orla Was Six* and *A Family Tree*, both of which are set in and around Belfast.

Ultimately, though, it is *Give Them Stones* that examines one woman's move from the nationalism that informed her childhood toward the recognition that women are used by all sides in the North. According to Beckett, women's needs remain unaddressed within Republicanism and nationalism, and by Northern Ireland and Britain. Thus women will begin to assert themselves by focusing on their need to clothe and feed their family, to interact and grow with other women, and to acquire financial and emotional independence. The women will also assert their desires by saying that they wish to be independent as *women* first, rather than nationalists.

In order to suggest the trajectory of Martha's move from a national identity to a gender-based class politics, this chapter examines the protagonist's initial adherence to nationalism in terms of that ideology's relation to internment. As Beckett herself has stated, the incarceration of generations has profoundly affected the familial and sociopolitical structure in Northern Ireland and must be fully examined if there is ever to be lasting peace in the region (Sullivan 1995, 11). This chapter also examines the protagonist's concern with class politics and urges us to explore Martha Murtagh's seemingly contradictory status as a worker and a business owner.

## Women and Nationalism in
## Northern Ireland: Some Refusals

The crucial scene in Beckett's narrative—a narrative which places fictional events in the context of historical and cultural moments—occurs when the officer of a local British command visits Martha's home-bake shop (bakery). In response to pressure from the IRA and to the surly attitude of military men sent to Belfast after England imposed direct rule (1972) over Northern Ireland, Martha refuses to sell bread to British soldiers. This refusal has implications for the remainder of the narrative, and as a result of it, the British officer questions Martha's identity: "'Are you a Republican' he asked and I shrugged. I was going to be a heroine but instead I said, 'I am a home baker'" (123). Because her brother *may* be a Republican and her father was interned, and also because she lives in (nationalist and Catholic) West Belfast, the officer predetermines Martha's political allegiance and thus assumes he is able to ascertain the reason for her perceived transgression, her refusal to serve the soldiers. Yet Martha refuses to sell bread to the soldiers at least in part because the IRA had already warned her that she should not let the officers into her shop. When the IRA visited Martha's shop and ordered her not to sell to the military, Martha stated that although she would be "glad to be rid of them [the British]," she could not turn away customers (122). Eventually, however, Martha does refuse to serve the soldiers. She does this for two reasons: first, she fears that the IRA will hurt the soldiers; second, she agrees to do what the IRA wants her to do, but on her own terms. Martha refuses to say that she is neglecting the soldiers because she is a nationalist. When the British ask her why she will not serve them, and when they assume it is because she is a nationalist, Martha is again subversive: Martha says that she is a home baker, or a woman worker, and not a nationalist.

In the past, Martha had not so readily eschewed either nationalism or Republicanism because she was raised as a nationalist. Yet Beckett's text begins by noting that Martha was born during the British General Strike (1926), thus encouraging a reading of her life in terms of the international socialism suggested by this work stoppage. This fact also foreshadows her move from nationalism to a politics informed by gender and class. Martha's father and uncle support the British strikers as workers, although they debate whether or not Irish workers should support British workers even in the name of class solidarity. Martha's father thinks they should, but until the scene where she refuses to serve the soldiers, Martha has remained resolutely nationalist and has not been overly concerned with class.

In fact, one of the protagonist's earliest memories is of walking on Cave Hill with her father. She tells us that the walks on Cave Hill were ostensibly undertaken so that she and her father could pick bilberries; however, these journeys soon became informal history lessons. Martha the adult repeats what she learns and thinks as a child: "Not so long ago Wolfe Tone had addressed a meeting of United Irishmen up these [hills] and told them Ireland was going to be free. I didn't like the stories about tribes attacking or being besieged but I loved listening to how Ireland was going to be free"

(18). Although Martha is uncomfortable with military violence, she hopes for a united Ireland.

Wolfe Tone was the Protestant founder of the Society of United Irishmen, the late-eighteenth-century democratic, antisectarian organization influenced by the ideals of the French Revolution; this organization often used the Cave Hill site for meetings. The members of the United Irishmen were Protestant and Catholic men who opposed the Act of the Union, and the fact that the organization was made up of upper-, middle-, and merchant-class men suggests it did not deal with issues of gender and class inequality. As is evidenced both by her childhood experience and by her later recounting of it, however, Martha does not become conscious of this inadequacy of the organization for quite some time; instead, she adheres to the nationalist ideology she has been taught. Although she never questions Wolfe Tone, Martha will later ask why women's needs are excluded from nationalism and Republicanism.

In *Give Them Stones*, Martha discusses the civil rights marches of 1968 and 1969 and notes that although she admires Bernadette Devlin, she would have preferred it if, during the marches, Devlin and others had spoken publicly of a united Ireland (117).

Bernadette Devlin McAliskey has always insisted upon the primacy of material concerns. In *The Price of My Soul* (1969), Devlin notes that the purpose of her autobiography is to explain how "the complex of economic, social, and political problems of Northern Ireland threw up the phenomenon of Bernadette Devlin" (vii). In her interview in Derry Film Collective's *Mother Ireland* (1988), Devlin's insistence upon attention to material conditions is evident when she discusses the fact that after the civil rights marches, women in Derry were still beset by gender inequality and economic strictures: "Women in Derry were still making three square meals a day and men in Derry were still eating them; women in Derry were still washing the dishes and men were holding up the corner at the bookie shop." Finally, at the 1994 Clar na mBan "Women's Agenda for Peace Conference," Devlin spoke about the peace process and the possibilities it did and did not afford women. She contended that women's lot in Northern Ireland would remain unchanged after conflict resolution unless structural—economic—alterations were forged in the present.

When Martha discusses Devlin and the marches, however, she is not yet concerned with material constraints. In fact, it is what she sees as Devlin's exclusion of nationalism in favor of class concerns that Martha dislikes. Yet we, the readers, recognize Beckett's disappointment with Devlin as an indicator of how loyal she is to nationalism; we recognize that her later refusal of nationalism in favor of feminism and class consiousness, then, is quite significant.

After her discussion of Devlin, when her somewhat more pragmatic sister Mary Brigid questions Martha's political loyalties, Martha is emphatic in her allegiance: "All Mary Brigid said was, 'You and your United Ireland! Are you always thinking about it?' 'No,' I said. 'I'm always thinking of baking bread and selling it and feeding my family and what they'll be when they grow up but the thought of the border's like a nail sticking up in my shoe. I've got used to it but it's never comfortable!'" (118). Here Martha's response does indicate her concern with material conditions but suggests that this concern has not yet taken precedence over her nationalism.

When she states that she is always thinking about how she will feed her children, Martha is referring in part to the fact that her husband, Dermot, does not contribute financially to the support of the family. Although Dermot does work as a delivery man, Martha acknowledges that he has been taught that his money is his own: "But Dermot had been spoilt. He thought his money was his own" (90). As a Catholic man in Belfast, Dermot has a tenuous relation to capital (he has not always been able to obtain employment); he is, nevertheless, a man and, therefore, has patriarchal privilege. The privilege extended to him as a man in a conservative, patriarchal society is evidenced by the fact that he does not (have to) share his pay with his wife. Thus Martha *must* consider how she will feed her family; but, at this time, her concern has not translated into a political consciousness that will enable her to parallel her role as the economic support for her family with her use by, and role within, Republicanism, nationalism, and the state. The patriarchal family, Republicanism, and the British and Ulster state all seek to use Martha's time and money for their own purposes; eventually, Martha will begin to resist this.

After the scene in which her allegiance is questioned by the British soldier, Martha does turn away from nationalism. Significantly, when Martha finally refuses to be identified as a nationalist, she is also rewriting the generally acknowledged reading of the General Strike. Indeed, while the fact that Martha is born in the year of the strike is meant to indicate the international socialism espoused by her father and demonstrated by the strike, Martha extends this reading to suggest that even international socialism is inadequate if it neglects women. Ultimately, though her birth suggests her connection with material conditions such as the strike, her life will insist on the relation between material conditions and women.

When the British Trades Union Congress called a general strike on May 3, 1926, the miners promised to maintain necessary services, but the British government immediately led nonstrikers to presume otherwise. The British state sent a convoy of 105 armed trucks, each with guards and escorted by two armed cars, to the London docks to load food. Also, Hyde Park was quickly converted into a milk distribution center. The home secretary (through the BBC) broadcast an appeal for thirty thousand extra volunteer special constables; the Home Office issued a communiqué about legal and constitutional powers; extra troops were ordered; and before the end of the strike, four thousand strikers were arrested, many of whom had not been issued a warrant. The BBC began to issue constant strike bulletins, and the strike itself was declared illegal in the House of Commons. Throughout, the BBC and the *British Gazette* (under the editorship of Churchill) solidified their role as propaganda for the state. Although the strikers maintained their promise of providing for essential services, the British state used excessive propaganda to incite hysteria against them.

Most scholars suggest that specific difficulties notwithstanding, the General Strike indicated the potential of class solidarity. Indeed, it was this class solidarity that frightened the state. Also, conventional Marxist readings indicate that the strike demonstrated both the British state's willingness to exert excessive force and the precariousness of Britain's imperial power (see John Foster). Those who have correctly connected the strike to the sympathy it received in Belfast have conjectured that Britain's response to the strike indicated how London would deal with Northern Ireland: in both instances, it would fail to listen to workers and would overplay the need for security and consequently incite workers' anger.

Yet Martha's rejection of nationalism reminds us that any ideology that "merely" demonstrates the repression of the state and highlights the need for worker solidarity will not alter women's predicament within capitalism and imperialism. Therefore, Martha's rejection of nationalism is simultaneously a rejection of the terms of the General Strike and similar movements that stress class solidarity but do not underscore change for women. Nevertheless, her birth during the strike does demonstrate the possibility of class and gender consciousness. Martha will ask not only how socialists might work with nationalism but also how a woman worker comes to terms with a nationalism that does not include her.

Informed by the General Strike, Martha's final rejection of nationalism is a recognition that for women, national identity has been that which predefines them, and that which allows paramilitary forces to mandate women's actions. Once she acknowledges how Republicanism as well as British colonization have encouraged her to foster an ideology not her own, Martha becomes conscious of her status as a nationalist and state commodity. She recognizes that nationalism is merely one link on the identity chain upon which women are the objects of exchange; as Gayatri Spivak explains: "Women can be ventriloquists, but they have the immense *historical* potential of not being (allowed to remain) nationalists; of knowing in their gendering, that nation and identities are commodities in the strictest sense: something made for exchange. And that they are the medium for exchange" (1992, 803). In "Acting Bits/Identity Talk," Spivak indicates that although one's desire/need to identify oneself is understandable, women are especially vulnerable to that version of identity formation/identity politics which is co-opted by the state and nationalist forces. Her theorizations of nationalism have also cogently argued that when this ideology is regarded as the *only* discourse replete with emancipatory possibilities, subaltern resistance is obscured. Spivak is aware, too, that the very nationalist forces that could alleviate the conditions imposed by colonization are often those forces that will oppress women during colonization *and* after independence (1988a, 245).

While Martha recognizes, in the scene where the British officer questions her political allegiance, that women's national identity is commodified, the extent to which both the British and Northern Irish state and Republicanism attempt to co-opt this identity is illustrated in two scenes that follow. In both scenes, Martha's workplace is harmed or destroyed *because* she wishes to be defined as a female wage earner rather than as a nationalist.

In the first scene, the British officer visits Martha for a second time. Martha has closed the shop for her brother's funeral and is questioned about this by the officer: "'Was it [the closing] a gesture of defiance?' he demanded. 'Listen you,' I said, 'it's my shop and my business and I'll open or shut as I please and nobody intimidates me'" (126). The officer then tells Martha that he knows her brother was in the IRA and that her father was previously interned. Although Martha never denies her brother's involvement in Republican activity, she does indicate that he never spoke to her of his participation in the IRA. Additionally, in 1941, Martha's father, like many other Catholic men, was interned for two and a half years for suspected Republican activity, even though the case against him was never proved. It is important that the officer mentions her father's internment, because it was after his incarceration that Martha left school and went to work. Finally, the officer leaves.

The next day, however, his men search and disrupt the shop. Because Martha refuses to be, as she says, intimidated, she is harassed by the soldiers. But this harassment occurs at the level of her status as a worker and business owner. It is her *shop* that the officers search thoroughly, not her house. Although the officers visit her home and harass her sons and husband, it is clear the shop is their primary concern. They first attack the shop, and they comb through it more carefully than they do the house. The state only wants Martha to be a worker if she will "work" for it: if she will provide information and be defined as the state wishes to identify her.

In the second scene, Martha's shop and then her home are destroyed by the IRA. In protest of the kneecapping of a young boy (and in defiance of the implied threat to her in this incident), Martha refuses to pay the protection money routinely collected by paramilitary forces. Because she refuses to pay the money and because she is protesting the shooting of the young boy, the IRA burns her shop; Martha describes IRA members' actions: "'We're to burn you out, Mrs. . . . we've our orders. We have to do what we're told. You know that.' And they asked did we want to get our clothes. 'And a few blankets, Mrs. It's cold out'" (144). Because she refuses to "work" for them (initially, to boycott the soldiers), and because she will not identify herself as a nationalist and a Republican, the IRA destroy Martha's workplace, thus disallowing her from defining herself as she chooses: as a worker. Because she refuses to be who they, for different reasons, want her to be, the British army and the IRA rampage and burn Martha's shop. They both harm her because neither of them want Martha to be a women worker; they only want her to be the nationalist they define her as.

Both of these scenes occur because Martha acknowledges the relations among British colonization, nationalism and Republicanism, and economic exploitation. She also recognizes how these ideologies attempt to co-opt women's national identities. Speaking of the Thatcher government's response to the hunger strikes of 1981, Martha aligns England's moral and legal jurisprudence with colonization and poverty: "The government in England with that stony-faced addiction to the '*rule of law*' which meant they could oppress for centuries the poorer people of Ireland and India and Africa for their own good" (141; emphasis mine).

As Martha sees it, the rule of law is British colonial rule, and it allows Britain to colonize poor people in Ireland and Africa and India. Yet it is not just British colonialism that enacts the rule of law; Martha's schema acknowledges that so too does the Republican movement. Martha speaks about the IRA within the context

of "law and order," thus equating its actions with British colonization, specifically Britain's rule of law: "I could do nothing about all
of that [British colonization and imperialism]. It was all out of my
reach but when the Provos [Provisional IRA] took it on themselves
to bring *law and order* to the district, I got angry" (141). Because
she critiques British colonization and Republican ideology, and
because she dares to suggest that colonization and Republicanism
are more closely aligned than one might initially imagine, Martha
is punished by the IRA: "I was well known for that view. So the
Provos chose to knee-cap that boy at the wall of my shop where the
sun had shone on me in the morning" (141).

The young boy who is shot in front of her shop is used as a
threat to Martha the female business owner and worker: if she
continues to critique Republican and nationalist ideologies, she
too will be punished. The boy's body—the now disciplined and
docile body of the youth who, as he is being shot, screams, "Don't
do it again. . . . Oh Mammy, Mammy I'm going to be good"—is
thus made analogous to the site of Martha's shop. The boy's body
*stands in for* Martha's bakery, and Martha the worker and business
owner is aligned with a "transgressive" youth, a young boy punished because he supposedly dares to step outside the boundaries
of Republican law and order. If she continues to disobey the IRA
and call herself a woman worker rather than a nationalist or Republican, and if she uses her shop to work, rather than as a place to
signal nationalism, then she will be punished. This "lesson" is especially significant when we acknowledge that for some women in
(post)colonial regions, their bodies are often the sites of their labor
power and also of their possible resistance to capital and colonial
domination (see Spivak, *In Other Worlds*). When the IRA threat-
ens Martha's shop/body, it acknowledges that it knows the way in
which a woman's body can be used by and for her; the IRA wants
to use Martha's body for its purposes.

Although in *Remarks on Marx* he has perhaps worked to distance himself from rather than contribute to Marxist theory, Foucault recognizes the distinct relationship between punishment and
the economy or, rather, between the need for a docile and disciplined body and the machinations of a political economy. Accord-

ing to Foucault, "this political investment of the body is bound up, in accordance with complex reciprocal relations, with its economic use; it is largely as a force of production that the body is invested with relations of power and domination; but, on the other hand, its constitution as labour power is possible only if it is caught up in a system of subjection. . . . the body becomes a useful force only if it is both a productive body and a subjected body" (25–26). By way of Foucault, we can see that both the boy's body and Martha's shop are used for (the IRA's) economic purpose. The boy's body is an example of how the IRA will discipline or subject one, and Martha's shop is that place they want either to make protection money from or to use as a nationalist site. In addition, if Martha insists upon defining herself as a worker rather than as a nationalist or Republican, she will be punished. This punishment is ultimately enacted (her shop is burned) when by refusing to pay the protection money, Martha refuses to *recognize* and *subsidize* Republican and nationalist ideology and continues to insist upon her status as an independent worker.

### Internment: Punishment, Power, and Class

In his discussions of punishment, Foucault examines one of the most patriarchal and repressive of all state institutions: the prison. In *Give Them Stones,* Beckett introduces the interrelationship of punishment, the political economy, and incarceration because Martha is introduced into the workforce after and because her father is interned. Between the crucial scene where Martha refuses to be defined as a nationalist or Republican by the British officer, and the scene where her shop is initially searched and then burned, Martha speaks of internment. Indeed, Beckett's positioning of internment is hardly accidental. This trope is placed *between* the two telling moments I have outlined, so Martha's rejection of nationalism in favor of her status as a female worker is contingent upon her recognition of how women suffer as a result of incarceration. When Martha's father was interned, Mrs. Murtagh toiled long hours and Martha went to work in the mill. Martha speaks of internment after she remembers the Falls Road Curfew and women's response to it.

After what has become known as the Falls Road Curfew of 1970—the curfew that is often assumed to have initiated and preceded the reintroduction of internment—Martha recognizes the injustice of the British army with respect to women. The Falls Road Curfew was instituted by the largely Unionist-controlled Stormont government in Belfast with the support of Westminster and was carried out by the RUC and British soldiers. The action was initially intended to quell nationalist unrest but was subsequently used as an opportunity to harass suspected Republicans (Jennings et al., 3).

When Martha watches the aftermath of the curfew on television, she voices her frustration for and pride in the women of Northern Ireland: "I was crying, first with vexation and then with pride when a whole *army of women with bread and milk* came marching down from other streets farther up [the Falls Road] and pushed the soldiers away, shouting at them to go home to England and learn manners. They handed the food in to the besieged houses" (121; emphasis mine). Here Martha becomes aware not only of the specific effects of oppression upon women but also of the specific resistance women will demonstrate. In the face of British colonization, women will mobilize their own army and "[hand] the food in to the besieged houses." Because she uses the word "army," Beckett indicates that many women will fight injustice by highlighting, and then working toward alleviating, material conditions: they will fight the British by creating an army of women who will feed one another. Women will be the soldiers, and food will be their sustenance. These women will not fight colonization with nationalism, but instead will demonstrate that it is on the material level that people are being most oppressed, and it is on this level that women will resist. Importantly, this equation between women and food suggests not women's essential role as nurturers, but rather that women here make the decision to counter colonization with sustenance.

That women resisted by bringing food into the besieged houses is important because when the curfew was declared, the British army prevented food vans from entering the area. Thus women from outside the area actually marched down the Lower Falls Road, through lines of soldiers, and brought milk and bread into the curfew zone; they were directly defying British orders. Furthermore, after women's initial and relatively spontaneous act of resistance, they organized a protest: On July 3, three thousand working-class women marched down the Falls Road carrying bread and milk. In "Struggling for Peace and Justice: Reflections on Women's Activism in Northern Ireland," Monica McWilliams states that the planned protest was "the first action specifically organized by women as women" and that the women were clearly identifying with each other as working-class women (1995, 21–22). When Martha watches the women bringing bread and milk to one another, she becomes more adamant that neither nationalist sympathy nor the British army will help women; she becomes politicized as a working-class woman.

Significantly, Martha becomes radicalized after she watches the women on television. Critics have recently begun to suggest the media's, but especially the BBC's, role in crisis containment in Northern Ireland. In "A Little Local Difficulty?: Public Service Broadcasting, Regional Identity, and Northern Ireland," Martin McLoone argues that the BBC has always contained the conflict in Northern Ireland and that it also assumes a unified national culture. McLoone persuasively argues that although it has espoused "impartiality" and a respect for "all communities" in the North, the media has reified difference and tension. He cites the BBC's decision with regard to the name of Northern Ireland's second-largest city: because many nationalists refer to this city as Derry, and Unionists often call it Londonderry, the BBC decided to use the designation Londonderry when the city is first mentioned in a broadcast and to thereafter call it Derry. The BBC considers that in this instance, it has made a compromise. The BBC is unselfconscious about the fact that this decision merely institutionalizes difference while maintaining the illusion of harmony and compromise. The broadcast Martha watches demonstrates, however, that the media cannot suggest peace here. She watches the broadcast and recognizes the class and gender inequality at work. Her later response will be to fight material injustice with material assistance; not unlike the women who march up the Falls Road bringing bread and milk to the besieged homes, Martha will bake bread for her poorer neighbors.

After the Falls Road Curfew, internment was reintroduced in August of 1971. IRA resistance emerged in response to internment, and it is this resistance that encourages Martha to eschew nationalism, because she resents IRA violence just as much as she opposes British colonization. Just before internment is reintroduced, Martha is forced to acknowledge IRA violence, again especially as this violence affects women: "A wee girl up the Falls Road was out for a walk with her doll's pram and her baby sister when the baby sister was shot and killed by IRA men shooting at soldiers" (124). When she begins to recognize that the particular effects of the IRA's call for a united Ireland were being felt by the women ("the IRA talked about 'accidents of war' but it sounded too glib and I felt ashamed, sometimes horrified" [124]), Martha tells us that internment is reintroduced. Again, she conceives of the horror of internment primarily as it will impact upon women: "All summer there was word of internment. . . . I was baking bread when it started. I heard the banging of bin lids and later on the shooting" (125).

As is generally recognized, women banged garbage can lids to warn men that British troops and RUC officers were approaching. Yet few people remember that the tactic of banging lids emerged from another kind of protest. In the 1950s, women banged lids to warn their families that the housing inspectors were making their surprise visits to the estates. The inspectors were particularly unwelcome because of their unpleasant demeanor and also because people feared that they would be punished or fined. Martha's focus on the women who banged bin lids, then, indicates her focus on their relation to internment and housing. Yet although Martha may marvel at the bravery of the women who bang lids, and thereby support nationalism by supporting their men, she recognizes that this participation in nationalism ultimately will not benefit them.

Early emergency legislation would have allowed the internment indicated in Beckett's text. Indeed, current powers of arrest, search, temporary detention (up to seventy-two hours without charge for interrogation), internment, and related powers such as the right to close roads, have been made possible in Northern Ireland by laws originally proposed in Britain, the Republic, and Northern Ireland during World War I (Jennings et al., 14). This original legislation—the Defense of the Realm Act—was repealed in Britain in 1920 but extended in Ireland under the Restoration of Order in Ireland Act of 1920 (14). The act not only extended British control over Ireland but also set the tone for what would be Britain's response to political protest on the island: the need for the "restoration of law and order." When, in 1922, Northern Ireland was created by partition, these laws were reenacted under the Civil Authorities (Special Powers) Act (Northern Ireland) of 1922. What was later known simply as the Special Powers Act became permanent in 1933 and was drafted to exclude risk of judicial challenge.

Eventually, after the dissolution of the Stormont government (1972), Lord Diplock was appointed to review security law and policy in Northern Ireland; his committee recommended not only the continuation of internment without trial but also a new system of special courts that would allow quicker convictions (Jennings et al., 7). The committee recommended a new package of laws that would allow for the following: military arrest and detention of suspects and internment of suspects for seventy-two hours pending a decision on prosecution, internment, or release; the suspension of a jury trial for terrorist offenses; and the admissibility of convictions based on confessions obtained by the army. This package became the Northern Ireland (Emergency Provisions) Act of 1973, and many believe that it was a combination of this package and the effects of "Bloody Sunday" in 1972, when thirteen unarmed civilians were killed, that bolstered IRA recruitment.

While the practice of internment or, more accurately, the reintroduction of internment, ended in 1975, much damage had already been done. "While internment operated, 2060 republicans as against 109 loyalists were detained, at a time when loyalist violence was as vigorous as that of nationalists" (O'Leary and McGarry, 197). Because internment largely targeted Republicans, IRA recruitment increased. Most significantly, however, history tells us that the reintroduction of internment has bolstered IRA recruitment and contributed to nationalist fervor. Beckett insists that some women used their anger about the injustice of internment to recognize and call attention to class concerns.

Martha's emphasis on women is strikingly familiar to contemporary literary, sociological, and ethnographic analyses of imprisonment, which acknowledge the difficult burden placed upon the women who are left behind. Although there are some female political prisoners and other women with criminal status, males comprise the majority of the prison population in Northern Ireland. In *Web of Punishment: An Investigation,* Carol Coulter states that according to the Northern Ireland Office, which administers Northern Ireland, approximately 14,220 people have been charged with a "terrorist type" offense between 1973 and October of 1990. There have been approximately 12,087 convictions over the past seventeen years, bringing the total number of family members impacted to 100,000 (Coulter 1991, 12). Since many prisoners are from working-class areas and small farms, family members, particularly wives/partners and children, must cope with the emotional and often the financial trauma of incarceration. Through interviews and research, Coulter examines how the women cope when the men they love are incarcerated. Women tell Coulter about the difficulty of traveling to prisons, the financial strain on families, and the difficulties of raising children alone. Coulter also explores the differences between loyalist and Republican families. Sinn Fein has a well-organized committee that deals with prisoners and their families. Loyalist communities, at the time of her writing, were just becoming similarly organized. Families that deny a political allegiance are often more alone in their journey. Yet according to independent reports, many prisoners and their families face similar problems.

In *Silent Sentence: Working with Prisoners' Families,* a report based on NIACRO's 1990 international conference on imprisonment and Northern Ireland, three primary areas of concern are indicated: the prison (the visiting experience, transferring prisoners, preparing for release); community reintegration; and the family (the effects of familial imprisonment on family members, especially women and children) (Gormally). According to the report, women have the primary responsibility of caring for the children and maintaining a relationship with a partner whom they see infrequently and never without state supervision. Similarly, children are often confused and angry; some may also be required to seek employment to help support the family and to take on other adult responsibilities, as did Beckett's Martha. In "Master and the Bombs" in *A Belfast Woman,* Beckett provocatively suggests that it is women who pay the dearest price when men are incarcerated. In this story, the narrator's husband "gives himself up" when the RUC finds a bomb in his schoolhouse. Not at all political, the schoolmaster did not plant the bomb but uses political detention as an escape from domestic responsibility.

In *Give Them Stones,* when Martha hears the banging of the lids, she continues to work, thereby indicating that for some women, working is an act of resistance. She also suggests the relationship between internment and material conditions such as employment.

### Women, Class, and Northern Ireland

Internment solidifies her childhood entry into the workforce and encourages her position as an adult female wage earner, but Martha's status as a worker is nevertheless complicated by her position as a business owner. In Marx's most celebrated formulations, the two—the worker (producer) and the business owner (capitalist)—are separate and distinct. In one of *Capital*'s crucial elaborations, Marx states that "whoever directly satisfies his wants with the produce of his own labor, creates, indeed, use-values, but not commodities" (48). The worker (producer) produces use-values if the object created is used/consumed by himself; the worker produces surplus labor for others (or, rather, the worker's surplus labor is appropriated by the capitalist). Marx also emphatically states in *Capital* that "the mode of production in which the product takes the form of commodity, or is produced directly for exchange, is the most general and most embryonic form of bourgeois production" (94). By this latter definition, Martha the business owner would *seem* to participate in bourgeois production: Her bread would appear to be a commodity, something made for exchange. However, because of her status as a Northern Irish female worker, Martha complicates the very terms of Marx's analysis for women in (post)colonial locations.

Martha's complicated status as both a worker and a business owner becomes evident when we read Martha's reasons for opening her shop in terms of Marxist-feminist extensions of class analysis. In one of the initial texts to question gender and western Marxist theory, Juliet Mitchell's *Woman's Estate* encourages a feminist theory of class that acknowledges women's peculiarly overdetermined status. When she speaks of her overdetermination, Mitchell is referring to the many cultural and economic considerations regarding a woman's construction. According to Mitchell, women's lot cannot be read in simple Marxist terms; it is more complex. For her, to acknowledge women's overdetermination would mean rejecting the idea that women's condition "can be deduced derivatively from the economy (Engels), or equated symbolically with society (early Marx). Rather, it must be seen as a specific structure, which is a unity of different elements" (100). Mitchell acknowledges the social construction of the sexes, which determines how women are viewed/constructed with reference to labor, the family, reproduction, and sexuality.

When we read Martha's story in terms of Marxist-feminism, we can see that her desire to become a worker and a business owner does not easily conform to the producer-capitalist relation articulated by Marx, but rather is a result of her peculiarly overdetermined status. Martha does not merely produce commodities for exchange and consumption; nor, strictly speaking, does she produce only use-values. Rather, in response to her position as a Northern Irish woman who wishes to feed her family, provide for other women, and redefine value, she produces what she sees as the bread of life because it sustains women.

If Martha's status must be viewed within what Mitchell terms a "unity of elements," the first element is that Martha must work within Northern Ireland's discriminatory employment practices; the other elements include Martha's identity as a woman and the fact that she is a Catholic in Northern Ireland. As is often acknowledged, pre-1972 and during the Stormont government, Catholic women and men were discriminated against. The initiative Martha demonstrates when she opens her shop is therefore commendable; interestingly, this initiative is made possible because of the money willed to Martha by her great aunts and also because of a loan provided by her mother. Martha's shop is established, then, with money made by women!

When the state and IRA disrupt and destroy Martha's shop, they are halting the productivity of women. They are not hindering the enterprise of one woman; rather, they are disallowing the work/production of the generations of females who have contributed to Martha's shop. They are also disrupting what Martha often does for poor women and children: give away her bread (102). After the rent strikes of 1969 (the strikes initiated by working-class Catholics in protest of employment discrimination and inadequate housing), the Stormont government contained civil protest, and Martha and other working women suffered: "The Stormont people decided that they'd take the rents out of dole or children's allowance or whatever they could get at and some people were really hungry. *I had to give out bread free,* time and time again" (130; emphasis mine). Furthermore, because of the government's disruption, Martha is unable to feed the women whom she so enjoys. "The women coming home in the evening called in to buy my bread and kept me late working but I looked forward to them—fat jolly women in a bunch with their fingers wrapped in bits of cloth from the cuts they gave themselves chopping up fruit [in the canning factory which only remained in operation for a short time]. . . . they were kind to me and . . . called me 'Martha love.' . . . they filled the need I had for neighbors" (102). When the British government and Republican paramilitaries disrupt Martha's business, they make it difficult for her not only to feed her family and provide free bread to the women who most need it, but also to enjoy the women's company.

The above analysis suggests alternatives to a facile reading of class analysis, a reading which would see all bourgeois production in terms of the relation between product and commodity and worker and capitalist. Martha's bread *is* a product, but because she often gives it away free, because she conceives of its sustenance in terms of the relations it allows between and among women, and because for her it is that which may alleviate her family's poverty, the bread cannot easily be defined only as a commodity or neatly be assimilated into bourgeois production. Neither can Martha herself be defined as only a worker or only a capitalist. Because Martha is a Northern Irish women, she works in an economy that discriminates against her, and she creates products that she often gives away for free.

In addition to providing an opportunity to interrogate the producer-capitalist binary and the definition of a commodity, Beckett's text forces a consideration of Marx's use-value and his ill-defined but significant concept "value." For Marx, "the utility of a thing makes it a use-value" (42), and this "use-ful" thing becomes significant through its use or consumption. A useful thing, accordingly, has value by virtue of the labor contained in it (45). By questioning value and "use-ful" things, *Give Them Stones* necessarily examines preconceived definitions of labor and consumption. When Martha initially conceives of her business, she thinks of it less in terms of monetary profit and more in terms of her desire to be productive in and for herself—to be a worker: "My mother and I had worked out a fair price for the bread. . . . I had a bit of money at the end of each week, not a lot. *I didn't take any account of my labour* and by the end of each day I was ready to drop. . . . For years I never had enough sleep but I didn't mind, really. It mattered more to me that I was managing" (101; emphasis mine). If we take her words literally, we see that Martha takes no account of her labor because she is not extracting only surplus value from her body. The Republican paramilitaries who punish a young boy to indicate the fate that could befall Martha, view her body in terms of the surplus value they can extract from it.

By taking no account of her labor, Martha eschews this formulation and simultaneously suggests that the labor of some women—especially (post)colonial women—may be defined less in terms of monetary profit and more in terms of economic and social consideration; these considerations are dependent on relations between women and on women's desire to provide for themselves and their families. I am not suggesting an essentialist reading of women, but rather an acknowledgment that when they are used by state and paramilitary forces and when they disagree with the ideologies proposed by them, some women will begin to redefine their material status within a (post)colonial region.

Marx's theories of labor assume that the cornerstone of the capitalist mode of production is based upon consumption and is thus reliant upon surplus labor: The capitalist can buy the labor power of the worker at its value and extract more than its value by forcing the worker to work longer; thus the capitalist can extract surplus value (through surplus labor). In *Capital,* Marx acknowledges the "technical and social" conditions of the process necessary for the conversion from necessary labor into surplus labor, but he assumes that the mode of production itself must be revolutionized by the capitalist in order for the productiveness of labor to be increased (345). Thus it is the *capitalist* and not the worker who encourages the "productiveness of labor"—the extraction of surplus labor and, eventually, value. Again in *Capital,* Marx indicates what determines value: the amount of labor socially necessary for the article's production (46). Although Marx assumes his theories are mired in material history and cultural contexts, he never conceives of the female worker who redefines value, nor one who encourages the production of labor for her own purposes. Martha takes no account of her labor and therefore refuses to equate labor time with value. Instead, she redefines value and useful articles by using what Marx would call surplus labor and applying it to sustain her shop and help other women. Her actions underscore Gayatri Spivak's much misunderstood assertion that value is not representative of labor (1988a, 158).

According to Spivak, value indicates difference: "What is represented or represents itself in the commodity differential is Value"

(158). While Marx sees "value" and "use-value" as interdependent, Spivak thinks use-values undo the determinacy of value. Thus use-values, whether they are things or labor or power, are changeable and become specific only in specific contexts. This is important for Spivak because it allows her to contend that if value is "attended to, then there is the possiblity of suggesting to the worker that the worker produces capital, that the *worker* produces capital because the worker, the container of labor power, is the source of value. By the same token, it is possible to suggest to the so-called 'Third World' that it *produces* the wealth and the possiblity of the cultural self-representation for the 'First World'" (1990, 96; emphasis in original). Mary Beckett's Martha is the source of value because she bakes for herself and other women; she takes no account of her labor and produces use-values for other women. When we read Spivak, we can see that Beckett's Martha makes it clear that women in Northern Ireland help produce the wealth and cultural self-representation of the army and paramilitaries and can therefore alter women's plight.

If we redefine value, women can argue for an elaboration of value and labor that is not tied to traditional concepts of commodity and capital, and which simultaneously reconsiders (re)production.

Complicating previous theorizations of the relationship between production and female (re)production, specifically Engels's analysis in *The Origin of the Family, Private Property, and the State*, Gayatri Spivak argues that the (post)colonial woman redefines value in its relation to her body. Spivak's theory cogently examines the woman whose body is the site of the convergence of the national and international sphere(s) of labor. In *In Other Worlds,* she critiques Eurocentric Marxist-feminists who discuss the reproductive labor of women while neglecting (and thus negating) the corporeal identity of the female. This allows her to highlight a transition from the domestic economy to another kind of domestic: the (post)colonial (mothering) maid servant; Spivak defines this transition as the move from "the domestic to 'the domestic'" (1988a, 248). This is the transition from the domestic/private home to domestic/public work and the international sphere(s) of labor. For

Spivak, the two domestics—the "public" and "private"—converge at the site of the female servant's (in her example, maid and wet nurse) body. In her theorization of the subaltern who marks the transition from the domestic to "the domestic," Spivak convincingly argues that rather than provide a transition from the domestic to civil, private to public, the site of the family (which converges upon the corporeality of the woman) indicates the emergence of value. Spivak's emphasis on the move from the domestic to "the domestic," and the redefinition of value this suggests, is particularly compelling for an analysis of Martha Murtagh, the female wage earner who owns a *home* bake *shop,* a structure whose very name suggests its inability to distinguish between the public and the private.

In *Give Them Stones,* Martha's body is the site upon which (re)production is problematized and value is again redefined. At one point in her narrative, Martha refuses to engage in sexual intercourse with her husband. As she explains, "My own enjoyment was far less than the terrors I had afterwards that I might be pregnant again. I was nasty to him many a time but he never held it against me, never took insult, always ready to try again until we had four boys. *Then I said no, never again"* (87; emphasis mine).

Spivak has argued that in an era of multinational capitalism, we need to redress two key concepts in Marxist analysis of women: the role of the state and reproduction. With respect to reproduction, she speaks of reproductive rights and insists that "all initiatives of population control or genetic engineering are cruelly unmindful of the dignity of reproductive responsibility" (1995b, 116). Reproductive responsibility, especially in (post)colonial locations, is always also about women's personal/economic choice. Because during the early 1970s contraception was illegal in Northern Ireland, and because she is a woman who has been interpolated by Catholic ideology, Martha cannot avail herself of birth control. Whereas in the past Martha has refused the Marxist concept of value and its relation to surplus labor by "tak[ing] no account of [her] labour," here she refuses to reproduce workers and thus indicates that her value will be differently defined: She will also define value by her status as a worker who refuses Republicanism and state intervention, but who will not, *so long as capital/patriarchal relations are in place in the form of nationalism, Republicanism, and (British and Northern Ireland) state intervention,* reproduce others who may be unable to assert a status of their choosing.

When Martha decides that she will no longer (re)produce, we could take this to mean that she simply does not wish to have more children. Yet her decision is actually much more complex. Martha did not open her shop until her own children were grown, and no doubt she recognizes that if she has another child, she will no longer be able to work. Also, when we read Beckett's text in terms of Martha's class consciousness, we can see how the protagonist's decision not to have children becomes a marker for a critique of production and value. What Martha refuses to (re)produce is not just children but workers. If, as Spivak suggests, for (post)colonial women, the emergence of value is made more clear at the site of the family, then Martha is choosing to keep her value vested in her identification of herself as a worker, not as a mother.

Spivak expands upon her theory of female reproduction and women's socialization within the economy. She indicates that male state and global forces that seek to control women's reproductive choices and power do so in order to "socialize" women's labor: labor power is a commodity to be controlled by others, so women will produce only what the state wishes them to. Martha recognizes this control; she knows that sexual activity will ultimately control her actions, because it will leave her encumbered with children. If she becomes pregnant, Martha will not be able to run her bake shop. If she has to give up her shop, both the state and the IRA will not be disappointed, but Martha will be, and so will her female neighbors/customers.

Although Martha Murtagh was early initiated into nationalism, her later encounters with state forces and paramilitary organizations encourage her to recognize the inefficacy of nationalist or Republican ideology for women. Indeed, Martha acknowledges that for Republicanism (and the version of nationalism that it espouses) and British colonization (as well as Northern Ireland state power), her national identity is merely a commodity. Ultimately, by refusing national identity and Republican allegiance, Martha indicates her status as a worker. As a "home baker" or female wage earner, she will bake her bread for the working-class women around her, thereby disrupting nationalist ideology and state intervention and complicating the terms of Marxist theory for women. In a particularly feminist rereading of Marx, Martha the worker and business owner can be seen to be providing bread (in this reading, the "stones" of the novel's title) for women and encouraging them to brandish these "useful thing[s]" as sustenance against the (post)colonial, capitalist, nationalist, and state forces that oppress them.

Martha's ultimate rejection of nationalism is echoed by other female characters created by women. These characters, too, question and sometimes ultimately reject nationalism in favor of an emphasis on material reality. Although Beckett's fiction suggests the importance of material conditions such as class and internment, Martha's insistence on her material needs and her conflict with nationalism is strikingly resonant in cinematic portrayals of women. As in Beckett's text, filmic portrayals of women in the 1980s and 1990s also focus on nationalist women's relation to internment and their insistence upon material conditions. Like Mary Beckett, the Republic and Northern Ireland's foremost female filmmaker, Pat Murphy, provides protagonists whose relation to internment may be subtle (in the case of *Maeve*) but is nevertheless significant.

# *Maeve* and *Anne Devlin:* Nationalism, Incarceration, and Feminist Film in Northern Ireland

There are no fewer than 21 persons of my family enjoying the festivities of the season in the prisons of Dublin. . . . of my [immediate] family there are imprisoned my father, mother, three brothers and three sisters.

(Pat Murphy, *Anne Devlin*)

The conventional expectations that govern the psychological peripeties of bourgeois-novel-type plots must just as often be dismantled, or at least suspended, and another set of relational premises, based on material circumstances and political exigencies and accounting for the possibilities of both treachery and trust, must be elaborated.

(Barbara Harlow, *Barred: Women, Resistance, and Political Detention*)

IN PAT MURPHY'S FILM *Maeve* (1981, codirected by John Davis), a young Belfast woman makes a return trip to her hometown from London. Here Maeve Sweeney struggles to reconcile her father's nationalism, her sister and her mother's stoicism, and her own feminism, a feminism enabled by her self-exile. In more than one scene, Maeve argues with her Republican ex-boyfriend, Liam, about the difficulties of both nationalism and (post)coloniality for women. She tells him that "men's relation to women is like England's relation to Ireland. You're in possession of us. You occupy us like an army." This remark indicates the direction Murphy's films will take: they will question women's relation to established ideologies such as nationalism and (post)coloniality. Yet each of her films will ultimately urge us to consider the distinct economic and cultural conditions women encounter as a result of such ideologies.

In her 1984 film *Anne Devlin,* Murphy focuses on the almost forgotten female participant in Robert Emmet's 1803 rebellion. When she is remembered at all, Anne Devlin is often referred to merely as "Robert Emmet's housekeeper." History has also heralded her for her suffering, thus reifying her status as a martyr for the nationalist cause rather than as a woman who questioned both patriarchy and nationalism. Historians can depict Devlin as a martyr in part because of Ireland's history of casting women as females who have suffered by giving themselves or their sons to the cause of Irish freedom. Yet, according to Murphy's film, Devlin's role as a person who suffered and asserted her independence does not fit neatly into established categories.

In Murphy's film, even after Devlin has been jailed and tortured, she refuses to confide in the British authorities any more than they already know about the uprising. After many of the male participants have confessed, however, Emmet tells Devlin to state what she knows and save herself; Emmet indicates that he does not want her "blood on his conscience." To this, she responds, "I'll not swear one word against you; it's not for you I did it." When Murphy's Anne Devlin refuses to recognize Robert Emmet, she does so primarily to indicate that for her, the rebellion is not about Emmet and his nationalist concerns, but rather about Anne's desire to alter gender and class oppression. Yet Anne's refusal to name Emmet is also a refusal to participate in colonial schemes of recognition.

When Emmet tells Anne to swear against him, he does so from the prison yard, where he has been placed by the prison authorities. Until that moment, Anne did not know Emmet was alive. Because he is frustrated with what he sees as Anne's lack of cooperation, the sadistic prison warden, Dr. Trevor, brings Emmet and Devlin together. Dr. Trevor sends Anne outside to the prison grounds while he and other state authorities watch to ascertain whether or not she will recognize Emmet.

Although her refusal to recognize Emmet is primarily a protest against his notions of the rebellion in favor of her own, this refusal also has the effect of subverting the recognition scene fabricated by the colonial power. Anne will refuse to recognize Emmet and thus assert her independence from and disregard for the British colonial regime as well as the male nationalists Emmet represents. *Anne Devlin* was the first feature film to be cast, crewed, and financed in Ireland. It was also the first film to take advantage of a new tax incentive scheme that allowed investors to avail themselves of tax breaks.

Murphy's *Maeve* and *Anne Devlin* indicate that film by and about women in Northern Ireland shifts Ireland's cinematic focus from an emphasis on nationalism to an analysis of the material difficulties women in this (post)colonial region encounter as a result of nationalist and/or Republican ideology as well as state and colonial intervention. As is explained in the introduction and first chapter of this book, material conditions are the economic and cultural effects of capitalism, patriarchy, and nationalism as well as (post)coloniality. These effects can result in economic deprivation, lack of reproductive choice, or familial incarceration, among other things. Significantly, although Pat Murphy examines the nationalist narrative, she does so only insofar as this narrative constructs and reifies economic and gender inequality as well as women's relation to the state through the prison system. Her films also remind us that no materialist and Irish cultural studies analysis of cinema can be complete without an examination of the institutional constraints of film funding itself.

## The Irish Film Industry

In *Cinema and Ireland*, Kevin Rockett and his coauthors construct a genealogy of film production in the Republic and Northern Ireland and speak specifically about what they term "Ireland" and "Irish film." This history progresses from the silent period, through the 1930s and documentary, to the establishment of an Irish film studio, and, finally, to contemporary challenges. Film was introduced into Dublin in 1896, and in 1909 James Joyce established Ireland's first permanent cinema. Yet as has become characteristic of film in the Republic and Northern Ireland, history and culture collided to make production difficult if not impossible: in addition to the general problem of films being made about and not by the Irish, material complications arose. Although the first Irish film company was founded in 1916, it was burned one month later in the Easter Rising, when Patrick Pearse and others tried to take over Dublin. The rebel leaders surrendered and Pearse and fourteen others were executed by a British firing squad. According to Rockett and his coauthors, postindependence Ireland used film to promote a particular version of Ireland, the new state, while British military and Irish business and religious pressure ensured that films would be heavily censored (1988, 40). In postindependence Ireland, film was sometimes nationalist (even propagandist) in context. Through years of struggle to create a particularly "Irish" film—one not infused with British and American conceptions of the island—filmmakers sometimes focused on the Irish civil war and Irish nationalist history. Thus it is perhaps not surprising that women were compelled to examine and take issue with nationalism when they began to create film.

Despite early and continuing difficulties, the 1970s and 1980s held promise for film in the Republic and Northern Ireland. In 1972 the Irish Film Workers Association was established; and in 1973 the Arts Act increased the Arts Council's financial powers. In

1979 the Republic published two bills: one was to regularize film studios, the other was the Irish Film Board Bill. In 1980 the Irish Film Board Act was passed, establishing, theoretically, the Irish Film Board, Bord Scannan na h-Eireann. This state agency operated with approximately IR£0.5 million per annum during 1981–87. The initial term of Bord Scannan was fraught with tension, however, as the first year it allocated funding, the Irish Film Board committed half of its budget to one film: Neil Jordan's *Angel*. Independent filmmakers and activists protested the fact that such a large portion of the budget was allocated to only one film. While I do not have the space here to examine Jordan's *Angel* in depth, I would argue that the film's failure to dismantle preconceived images of Irish women is partially what made it recognizable and acceptable to the Film Board and to an international audience.

In 1985 a newly configured Film Board reconvened, and proposals for Ireland's film archive and the Irish Film Centre were set in motion. Grants and loans were made available through a statutory Irish Film Board, and in 1987, the Finance Act (Ireland) created tax incentives for private investors. Section 35 of that act allowed IR£600,000 to be invested by a company over a three-year period, and this investment could be deducted from a company's profit. The investment could not comprise over 60 percent of a film's total budget; also, 75 percent or more of the production work had to be completed in Ireland; another scheme would allow an investor to receive a onetime deduction for a contribution (Rockett et al. 1994, 129). As important as these schemes were, one week after the initial tax plan was unveiled, it was announced that the Film Board was being closed as part of the government's austerity program. In its initial six years, Board Scannan had been allocated IR£3.06 million and had funded a small number of feature and short films, as well as documentaries for television (Rockett et al. 1994, 128–29).

Despite this difficult beginning, there have been significant signs of progress in the Republic. In 1993 the Finance Act allowed for changes to section 35: there was an increase in the amount of money that could be invested in a film; the Business Expansion Scheme allowed for a larger individual investment; and section 35 was also expanded to include coproductions (Rockett et al. 1994, 131). In addition, according to an editorial in *Film Ireland,* the following advances have been made: the Irish Film Centre opened its doors (September 1992); Michael D. Higgins was named minister of the arts, culture, and the Gaeltacht (Irish-speaking region) (January 1993), though he no longer occupies this position; the Film Board, Bord Scannan na h-Eireann, was reactivated (March 1993); and the Irish Film Institution and Irish Film Centre merged to create the Irish Film Institute (June 1993). Other significant interventions include the new burst of student filmmaking, RTE's (Radio Telefis Eireann) commitment to independent film, and the Arts Council's establishment of a film script award (Rockett et al. 1987, 128). As of the early 1990s, animation production had increased, but a large percentage of film and television drama still came from outside Ireland (Rockett et al. 1994, 135).

While cinema in the Republic of Ireland has had a tumultuous history, in the 1990s film production in Northern Ireland is even more complex. When she analyzes whether or not there is a film industry in the North, Geraldine Wilkins states that the "relationship between film-makers in Northern Ireland to the industry in the Republic or Great Britain is the key to this question" (143–44). Northern Ireland film production, then, is necessarily informed by filmmakers' relations to the Republic as well as to Great Britain and even the United States. (The London, New York, Los Angeles connection emphasizes Hollywood film and thus sets the tone for what kind of cinema is commercially viable.) Writing in 1994, Wilkins sees some possibilities in the 1989 establishment of the Northern Irish Film Council; in 1992 NIFC began to receive government support through the Department of Education and, according to Wilkins, has "been concerned to encourage the development and understanding of all aspects of film, television and video in the region" (141). She also notes that filmmakers in Northern Ireland should be able to avail themselves of MEDIA funding. (MEDIA is the European Union program established to promote indigenous European film and television.) Finally, Wilkins productively suggests that "a vigorous industry in the south, stimulated by government support, can only benefit writers, film-makers and crews across the island as a whole" (144). She is encouraging cross-border production and cooperation.

In 1988 the Northern Ireland regional group of the Independent Film, Video and Photography Association stated that the main problem for those people trying to work in Northern Ireland is that the Arts Council of Northern Ireland (ACNI) is totally lacking in a policy for developing film and video. It claims that it has taken this position because of the attitude of the British Film Institute in refusing to recognize Northern Ireland under its constitutional remit (Independent Film, Video and Photography Association, 37). Ultimately, the Independent Film, Video and Photography Association calls for a merging of "art and industry" in the North (37).

As burdensome as financial concerns have been and continue to be in the Republic and Northern Ireland, film by women suggests other battles with which they must contend. While film production in Ireland has been difficult to sustain generally, it has been an area particularly challenging for women. Beset by the peculiarities of a patriarchal, (post)colonial history, seditious religious ideologies, and a complex relation to multinational capitalism, Irish women have always had to work with and against oppressive structures, thus making it more difficult for them to get films made. Also, women filmmakers still battle others' stereotypes of them. In my interview with Pat Murphy (1994), she noted that when she discussed a film script with possible financial backers in Germany, they said, "That's not what women in Ireland are like." They did not recognize the way Murphy had portrayed women because they only knew the uncomplicated images long fed to audiences by some men and/or filmmakers outside Ireland.

Beginning in the 1980s, the extent to which female filmmakers were challenging economic and nationalist forces was demonstrated cinematically, and one material condition that became a focus for Irish women filmmakers was the prison. For the reasons already discussed, and also because the women's relationship to the prison indicates how their needs are left unmet within nationalism and by the state, the site of the prison continues to assert itself in the films of Murphy and female filmmakers who follow her.

# Maeve

In 1981 John Davis and Pat Murphy's *Maeve* was funded by the British Film Institute and RTE; according to Murphy (1982), it was the first feature ever shot and cast entirely in Belfast. The film was funded largely by the British Film Institute; the BFI put £73,000 toward the production, while RTE contributed £10,000. In an interview with the Irish film critic Patsy Murphy, Murphy explains that although she was raised in Belfast, in 1972 she emigrated to England. In London, where she attended the Royal College of Art, Murphy enrolled in film classes. One of these was a course in "Oppositional Cinema," and the subject was Northern Ireland. Murphy was the only Irish person in the class, and she watched with horror films such as *The Informer,* which relied on traditional stereotypes, and newsreel footage of the North. It was then that she decided to make *Maeve* (Patsy Murphy, 1982). The film did not have a general release and was screened at the Irish Film Theatre. Maeve was played by Mary Jackson, Brid Brennan was Roisin, Trudy Kelly played Eileen; Mark Mulholland was Martin, and Liam Doyle was played by John Keegan. *Maeve* was Murphy's second film; *Rituals of Memory,* a film created from a scrapbook her mother sent her when she was in London, was Murphy's first film, and it was produced in 1977.

In *Maeve,* Murphy is keen to wrench the camera away from patriarchal representations of women; she also wishes to demonstrate that people in Northern Ireland must be more than merely the subject in the documentaries of others. Experimental in construction, *Maeve* complicates preconceived notions of documentary and feature film altogether, with the entire film shot in flashbacks that question teleological narratives of memory.

Murphy wants to call attention to how we remember an event, and how others construct and broadcast the troubles. As Kevin Rockett and his coauthors note, this film demonstrates both the significance of the narrativization of personal and social history and memory, and the constructedness of history and memory on a technical (filmic) level (1988, 139). Claire Johnston views this experimental technique as explicitly tied to feminist politics. She terms Murphy's technique "interventionist" (55) and argues that *Maeve* remedies history's disavowal of woman by carving "an imaginary for women which would enable them to enter history on their own terms, through the mobilisation rather than the underwriting of identification process" (56). Rather than merely conform to established representational modes of identification, women create new modes. Still other critics insist that Murphy's emphasis on narrative demonstrates that memory is inextricably bound to constructions of Irish history. Luke Gibbons contends that *Maeve* teaches us that in Irish culture, representations of narrative do not merely describe but rather also construct what it is that they claim to represent. Although it is true that all cultures construct representation, Gibbons views the Irish instance as particularly anomalous because its constructions have been used to foreground a political agenda.

One political narrative in *Maeve* is the story of Queen Medbh (Maeve), the mythical warrior queen of Connacht who gives the film its title. In the Irish saga the *Tain Bo Cuailgne,* Ulster is invaded by Medbh, whose mythical status emerges not only because she is unafraid to conquer territory but also because she confers kinship upon the men who sleep with her. But as the goddess of her territory, Queen Medbh indicates the significance not only of landscape, but also of gender, in Irish film. Because of this intertextuality, the significance of Maeve's right to claim her territory is a rewriting of traditional films, which explore the relation between landscape and the Republic or Northern Ireland but leave gender issues relatively unexamined. Murphy's *Maeve* indicates a reconsideration of traditional nationalist film in part because her Queen Medbh not only revisits her territory but also encourages an examination of the ideologies through which she has been interpolated: nationalism, feminism, Republicanism, and class.

These critical readings of *Maeve* correctly indicate the film's emphasis on gender and nationalism. Yet because each reading still strives to ascertain the link between the film's narrative and history in the Republic and Northern Ireland, each fails to recognize what perhaps most needs foregrounding: that *Maeve* indicates the failure of historical readings of nationalism to recognize the confluence of gender and material conditions.

Although on a narrative level the film is concerned with Maeve Sweeney's return from London for a visit to her native Belfast, the film uses flashbacks to underscore how Maeve's feminist politics initially complicate and ultimately take precedence over her nationalism. Each flashback suggests not only how nationalism has excluded Maeve but also, more specifically, how material needs have shaped her feminism. One such material need concerns the site of the prison. In what I am terming here the "prison scene," Maeve hears her uncle and other men discuss her father's incarceration and ridicule her mother, the woman who Maeve says "kept the family together" while Martin Sweeney was in jail. This flashback is particularly important for it prompts Maeve to tell her boyfriend she wants to leave Belfast. The prison scene reminds her of the inadequacies of a nationalist ideology in whose name people are imprisoned in the first place.

Maeve and her Republican ex-boyfriend, Liam, visit a Republican pub. In an interesting comment on the influence of the media (especially television) on the changing face of Northern Ireland and on the political control of a community, when Maeve and Liam enter the bar, their images and the images of the pub are seen by the audience as projected onto a television screen. The television serves as a camera monitor, and we watch as the two are frisked and the doorman looks through their belongings. The doorman conducting the search does not appear to be a member of the Northern Ireland security forces, but is probably a Republican, searching to be sure that no one is entering who could be a threat to the establishment or the patrons within it. Interestingly, although in Northern Ireland technology is often used by the security forces against perceived political dissidents, in this scene, the people use technology for their own purposes.

In the pub/prison scene, Republicans rely upon technology; they use it as a surveillance against "outside" intrusion and, significantly, against their own community members. The television camera reminds the film audience not only that people in

Northern Ireland are often watched (the theme of being watched courses throughout the film as television sets, surveillance cameras, and news programs abound) but also that people counter being watched by watching others, particularly women. Images of Maeve and Liam are projected on the television screen, foreshadowing and constructing their status as outsiders. Liam is an outsider to the Republicanism of Maeve's father's generation, while Maeve is an outsider to the Republican and/or nationalist ideology which excludes women, as well as to the version of feminism lived by her mother and sister.

Maeve's mother, Eileen, and her sister, Roisin, live a feminism that contrasts with Maeve's. When Maeve and Roisin discuss feminism, Roisin argues that she has "been to some of your meetings," and that she "does not have any trouble getting along with women." Her sister's responses indicate that Maeve's meetings failed to appeal to Roisin's particular, day-to-day concerns, while her declaration that she does not have any trouble getting along with women is meant to quiet Maeve's concern for female solidarity. This scene is juxtaposed with one where Roisin does indeed have female friends, while Maeve notes that she no longer has companions in Belfast. At the conclusion of the film, Maeve, Roisin, and Eileen do form a trio of solidarity against the male stories and nationalist narratives that surround them; however, their solidarity is fragile and can be (and is) interrupted by outside forces. Though critics often contend that the male bard who interrupts Maeve, Roisin, and Eileen on the Giant's Causeway in the penultimate scene is portrayed as comical and ineffective, he nevertheless is present; his voice may be ineffectual, but it is still there. In other words, feminist solidarity is possible, but it must contend with the rantings of an ineffectual yet still present patriarchy. In Northern Ireland, Maeve's brand of feminism may be gaining in strength and the patriarchal forces may be loosing their hold and power, but they are not yet defeated.

Perhaps one of the most interesting stories that emerges in the film, however, is Eileen's and Roisin's separate recounting of one of the presumably many times they have been stopped by a soldier. Although Roisin and Eileen both underscore the rudeness of the soldier, they also insist that it was Eileen's behavior that was unusual. Commanded to get out of the car, Eileen remains seated. The officer responds, "Didn't you hear me Missis? Get out of the fucking car." According to Roisin, Eileen "leapt at him" and shouted, "You are just a boy; you are just out of nappies." "If I was your mother, I'd slap your backside." The officer, initially stunned, appears to want to strike Eileen, but finally he begins to calm down as another soldier steps in. The significance of this story is that it highlights the particular challenges for women in Northern Ireland, women for whom Maeve's version of feminism may be inappropriate.

Although for Maeve the answer is to extricate herself from a region and an ideology that she finds oppressive, Roisin and Eileen maintain these ties. They may be unhappy with some of the effects of nationalism and patriarchy, and they may even dislike Belfast at times; nevertheless, they do find comfort in a version of nationalism, and they do consider Belfast their home.

In another scene, Roisin tells Maeve about a party she attended. At this party, Roisin and her friend retired to bed early. The front door to the house was open, and a British soldier walked in and came into the bedroom. He climbed into bed with the two young women and announced that he had not seen his wife in six months; he told the women to "make up your minds, then, which one of you is it going to be." The women ran out screaming and the soldier left, but although Roisin has obviously been frightened by the incident, she does not view it in the same terms that Maeve does. Maeve condemns the soldier but also wonders to what extent living in Belfast has shaped Roisin's sexuality. What Maeve fails to see, however, is not only that Roisin was able to extricate herself from the situation, but also that she does recognize the injustice of the soldier's behavior. Roisin, however, will contend with this injustice differently than will Maeve.

Yet the prison/pub scene indicates how much of an outsider Maeve is in this male-dominated Republican pub. If the stories that filter through the film have been constructed by Republican and nationalist ideologies, this scene demonstrates that although Maeve is continually watched, few want to recognize the hardships she, her mother, and her sister have had to endure in the name of these ideologies.

Although the pub scene begins with a reference to a nationalist narrative—the Republican bar checks people for security purposes and then projects their images onto a television screen which acts as a monitor—it quickly moves toward a comment on the materialist politics of imprisonment. Once she is inside the pub, Maeve recognizes her uncle and turns to leave; Liam convinces her to stay. As Liam and Maeve order their drinks, they are approached and invited to sit with the uncle and his cronies. The two sit at the table quietly as the men discuss local occurrences, and this litany of present events quickly leads them to discuss and reinvent past history. Soon we see Maeve's face, and although we do not initially view the other men we hear speaking, we do see men projected onto the mirror behind Maeve. These figures in the mirror are not the men sitting at the table with Maeve, but we are left with the impression that they *could* be; that is to say, the men telling their stories of the past could be almost any group of Republican or nationalist men in the pub. The stories "mirrored back" to Maeve through history are told by nationalist and Republican men and exclude Maeve and other women. Maeve's relation to the mirror here complicates dominant feminist film theory.

British and American feminist film theory is markedly influenced by Jacques Lacan, and Lacan's reading of the gaze is informed by and itself reverses the work of Jean-Paul Sartre. In *The Four Fundamental Concepts of Psycho-Analysis*, Lacan expounds his theory of the gaze and illustrates how it differs from Sartre's. According to Lacan, "The gaze, as conceived by Sartre, is the gaze by which I am surprised" (84). For Sartre, the gaze orders his world but cannot be seen: "In so far as I am under the gaze, Sartre writes, I no longer see the eye that looks at me and, if I see the eye, the gaze disappears" (84). Lacan disagrees. For him, the gaze is imagined, but it cannot be owned: "The gaze sees itself—to be precise, the gaze of which Sartre speaks, the gaze that surprises me and reduces me to shame, since this is the feeling he regards as most dominant. The gaze I encounter—you can find this in Sartre's own writing— is, not a seen gaze, but a gaze imagined by me in the field of the

Other" (84). Indebted to Lacan, feminists recognize that the gaze exerts power but usually insist that although this power is recognizable as the patriarchal unconscious, it is not "owned" by anybody in particular.

Although Trinh T. Minh-ha speaks of the (post)colonial condition, her work, too, remains mired in a version of film theory that fails to critique Lacan's disavowal of ownership. How would we read *Maeve* if we analyzed it in the context of Lacan and an identifiable gaze? Trinh T. Minh-ha speaks specifically of filmmaking and (post)colonial women. In *When the Moon Waxes Red: Representation, Gender, and Cultural Politics,* she provocatively names those who "own" the gaze; yet even hers is a general ownership. Throughout the essays in her collection, Trinh uses the words "him," "Master," and "them." In one essay she defines this terminology: "When speaking about the Master, I am necessarily speaking about both Him and the West. Patriarchy and hegemony" (148). To the extent that she names specific places and ideologies, Trinh disrupts film theory that, because it is informed by Lacan, fails to name the owner of the gaze. Yet she is too general and fails to acknowledge particular culpability.

Murphy's film recognizes the need for a materialist reading of the gaze, one which is unafraid to acknowledge not only that the gaze is owned, but also that the gaze, and the power inherent in it, can indeed be traced back to a specific "other" (in this case, Republican men). When the camera in *Maeve* moves from the men sitting at the table to the men seated throughout the pub, it does not fail to assign ownership to the gaze; instead, it suggests that the surveying gazes in the room are "owned": they are simply owned by more than one man, or, rather, they are owned by all the men who comprise the Republican movement. The gaze is attributed to Republican men and to state and paramilitary apparatus, all of whom are signified by the television and the reflections in the mirror. Thus, unlike a version of feminist film theory that does not assign ownership to the gaze, Murphy's film does; it proceeds so far as to suggest those who are responsible for the effects of the gaze upon women.

When the camera pans the pub, we hear the uncle's voice, and his narrative usurps the previously privileged voice of Maeve's father as the film's first narrator. Initially, as her uncle speaks, we still see only Maeve and the image of other men projected in the mirror behind her; it is not until her uncle's voice has been established and connected with the images in the mirror behind Maeve that the camera pans to him. Although her uncle will eventually speak about Maeve's family, he begins by giving the details of his own soured marriage, an account that establishes a bond between him and his friends; misogyny and nationalist politics merge. The men are misogynist because they use their distrust of women as a precursor to their Republican activity: women are the source of anger; Republicanism, the outlet for it. The uncle explains:

Uncle: I never was what you might call involved in the movement [Republican movement]. I never realized how much you wanted to put who you was all behind you until I got married. Dead respectable she was, ha. [She] lived off the Ormeau Road.

His friend, seated next to him: Right Bitch.

Another friend: Bloody puke.

Uncle: She moved out to the housing estate back and beyond. . . . I used to bring the wee daughters around to see their mummy. Give her a few bob at Christmas.

First friend: Ah fair play, fair play.

Uncle: All that stopped when she died. I never saw them from one end of the year to the next.

First friend: I know. I know.

Together, the uncle and his friends speak derisively about a woman whose side of the story we never hear. Presumably, the uncle's friends have heard this story before, but they listen again as he first vents his frustration and then uses this frustration to speak of his involvement in Republican politics. Furthermore, the narrative the uncle uses to speak about his deceased wife will indicate how he will interpret and then construct Maeve's mother. The uncle resumes his story:

Uncle: Anyway. [Short silence] In the middle of the 50s [IRA bombing] campaign, remember that? One time I had a box of jollies [incendiary devices] in the house. The peelers [British soldiers] made a search of the area. Colin and me had a great idea. We drove over to Glengormy and buried the box under the floor-bed in your man's house. We figured with him being respectable and all, who'd suspect him? But didn't the neighbor look out the window and get suspicious of two fellas . . . called the peelers. By that time we got away [pause]. Nobody believed Martin. He got a year in the Crumlin Road [jail] [laughter]. She, the wife, nearly left him. Must have thought he was up to something. [Music from pub players begins to gain momentum, and we hear the drum beat more forcefully].

Maeve: That's my father you're talking about.

First friend: Ach. Sit down! It's only a bloody story.

Maeve (to her uncle): You did that to your own brother, and he never told on you.

Uncle: She's right you know. He could've turned his back on us. Martin never was an informer. *She* [Maeve's mother] might have told though; only she was so scared.

Maeve: It was her that kept us together when he was in prison.

Uncle: Jesus. [Turns away from Maeve in disgust and perhaps embarrassment]

First friend: Ach. Shut up, Jesus. Would you shut up?

Maeve smashes the pints on the table and runs out of the pub. Liam runs after her and tells her that she must forget the past.

Maeve: Leave me alone. [Those] fucking bastards. I have to get away from here. I have to go *now.*

Liam: O.K. I'll leave my Da's house; I'll get a flat tomorrow. You can't let them get to you. You've got to forget the past.

The two embrace as Maeve cries silently. Liam supposes that the answer is for him to move into his own flat, presumably so that the two can have more time alone, and for Maeve to forget what has happened. For Maeve, however, the problem is much more acute: she wants to leave Belfast, its stories, and its memories behind.

Although one of the uncle's cronies encourages Maeve to "sit down" and states that "it's only a bloody story," Maeve realizes that these (nationalist) tales are indeed more than "bloody stories," because they help construct a myth and a history that excludes her and other women. These men literally try to suppress the voice of and role played by women whose husbands and fathers have been imprisoned for suspected Republican activity. Just as some Republican men try to exclude women's stories from the narratives of illegal activity and imprisonment, so too will they endeavor to exclude women from nationalist history more generally. They will also fail to recognize or examine women's material needs: they do not want to hear how Maeve's mother "kept the family together" economically or emotionally. When we read narratives related to incarceration, we can see not only how women are written out of nationalist history but also how their material needs are delegitimized. Unlike Liam, Maeve sees no way to forget the past; rather, Maeve assumes that the past comprises the present. Just as in the past Maeve's mother and her contribution to the Republican cause was forgotten, so too Maeve's words and feelings are not acknowledged. Indeed, the men of her father's generation (those who represent an older Republicanism) try to silence her, while the newer generation (Liam) says it understands but does not.

Liam does not understand how the past continues into the future, and he fails to recognize why Maeve needs to leave Belfast. Later in the film, when he goes to visit her in London, Liam tells Maeve that he knows not only why she left the North but also when she made the decision to do so. Liam twice asks Maeve why she left Belfast and moved to England and then answers his own question. "I'll tell you why you came. I know the exact moment. Remember that night coming home from the pub, when the Brits came along? They started with their questions: 'What's your name?' 'Where are you going?' and all that. You were scared 'case I'd do something. I could feel your shame because at the same time you wanted me to stand up for myself. . . . they threw me into the truck and what did you do? You ran home and got my fucking ma. Not my da; my fucking mother. You could have gone either way there but you decided to get out."

Liam retells a story that is more about him than it is about Maeve. He is the subject of this story, and Maeve's peripheral status is belied by the fact that Liam presumes to have already deduced her history from it. Furthermore, because some women in Belfast identify with the goals of Republicanism and nationalism, Liam believes that these ideologies are good for women. He thinks that Maeve is simply selfish when she suggests otherwise. What Maeve recognizes, however, is that Republicanism and nationalism cannot meet women's needs. She insists that this will become clear one day to Republican and nationalist women: "They've demanded that the aims of the revolution include them, and when this war is over and their position is still the same, they'll recognize you as the next stage in their struggle." But this realization does not serve as the catalyst for Maeve's departure from Belfast; rather, that catalyst is the prison/pub scene.

The prison/pub scene is particularly significant because it illustrates two points: (1) the inadequacies of a nationalist and/or Republican narrative for women (Maeve's uncle's version of what men do for the cause renders women peripheral at best, the objects of censure and derision at worst); and (2) the material effects of life in Northern Ireland for young women. It is the only scene where Maeve speaks of her desire to leave Belfast, and it is here that her feminist politics are established as a direct result of that which she has seen other women, especially her mother, subjected to. Because she has seen what her mother endured in the past, and because she recognizes that in the present Republican men refuse to acknowledge what her mother did, Maeve wants to leave Belfast; she knows that she will have no place or be recognized there either. Maeve identifies with how her mother's material needs and sacrifices have been ignored.

In *A Web of Punishment: An Investigation,* Carol Coulter acknowledges the difficult burden placed upon Republican and loyalist women when their husbands are imprisoned. She discusses prison sentences and states that "meanwhile the families, especially the wives, struggle to maintain their relationships with the prisoner and to keep a home for their children. But they all find it difficult, and not all survive" (1991, 92). Coulter's study is a collection of interviews, historical information, and analyses, and several of the people she interviews suggest that while there are difficulties specific to the particularities of a prisoner's sentence (that is, whether the sentence is long term or life, short term, or, perhaps most difficult, a sentence served in Britain), many family relationships are discontinued during this time, and many couples separate after the prisoner's release. The effects of familial imprisonment are also likened to grief, each stage of which requires its own resolution. Thus when the protagonist in *Maeve* suggests that her mother is the one who "kept things together" while the father was incarcerated, she is correctly assessing the role of the prisoner's wife, but she is perhaps obscuring the specific difficulties that a young daughter of a prisoner may encounter. Again Coulter discusses the situation and reads the work of psychologists who have written on the North and who note that "when the legally sanctioned punishment takes the form of incarceration, the concept of individual punishment for individual law breaking collapses. Children become caught in a web of punishment" (quoted on 21). Although for Coulter this statement indicates the psychological effects of familial imprisonment on children, I suggest that psychological repercussions are coupled with and often result in an altered material situation.

No doubt there are psychological ramifications of familial imprisonment, but the prison/pub scene in *Maeve* focuses more specifically on the material effects; in response to familial imprisonment, Maeve becomes angry at the nationalism espoused by the men at the pub because she recognizes that it is this version of nationalism that kept her father in jail and necessitated her mother's hardships. Finally, if, as Coulter and others suggest, children's involvement in familial imprisonment forces a reconsideration of the concept of individual punishment, *Maeve* indicates that prison narratives also speak to the inadequacy of reading texts merely for signs of individual growth and actualization. These psychological considerations must be read in conjunction with (and sometimes as subservient to) material conditions. As Barbara Harlow notes in her analysis of contemporary prison narratives, "The conventional expectations that govern the psychological peripeties of bourgeois-novel-type plots must just as often be dismantled, or at least suspended, and another set of relational premises, based on material circumstances and political exigencies and accounting for the possibilities of both treachery and trust, must be elaborated" (60). To read *Maeve* only or principally in terms of a protagonist's psychology is to fail to recognize the material consequences of incarceration and Republicanism for women. The prison scene forces a rearticulation of the concept of individual consequences for individual actions, while demonstrating the specifically gendered effects of collective and individual incarceration.

In addition to her analysis of the psychological effects of imprisonment upon family members, Coulter examines the class context of incarceration. She contends that children's ability to "accept" the fact of familial imprisonment in Northern Ireland often depends on whether or not these children have a broad-based family support network as well as community approval. Because of the nature of political crime in Northern Ireland, familial support networks often assume the role of extended family groups, while community approval is often made more possible in working-class areas, where there are signs of resistant activity and state control is most restrictive. In Maeve Sweeney's case, it would appear that her community has not been supportive. Maeve's uncle calls Martin Sweeney "respectable" and notes that he and his partner hid the jollies in a housing estate where they did not suspect the police would search. Therefore, the neighborhood was not working-class (although after they are burned out of their house, the Sweeneys do move to a working-class area). Thus Maeve may very well not have received community acceptance.

Scholars have stated that for prisoners' families, coping with children is a primary concern. Also significant is the degree to which the spouse is dependent on the child for support (Coulter 1991, 27). Maeve is the eldest in her family and may have felt some of this responsibility. She does think she has to protect her sister (although later in the film Maeve must accept that her sister is well able to care for herself, albeit in her own manner, a manner perhaps appropriate to life in Belfast). When they are young girls,

Maeve hits a boy after he punches Roisin and calls her a "Taig." As an adult, Maeve has seemingly become the more "practical" of the two sisters. Maeve arrives home from London and realizes that her sister has given her mother a present for her parents' anniversary, a gift which perfectly coincides with the decor of the sitting room Mrs. Sweeney designed to entertain the gentlemen she assumed her daughters would someday bring to the house. Maeve tells her mother that she was going to buy her something for the anniversary but decided to wait until she could ascertain what her mother needed. Maeve wants to be practical and mature in her selection. Maeve's maturity, however, does not prepare viewers for Murphy's *Anne Devlin*, who is herself imprisoned.

### *Anne Devlin*

Significantly, although in *Maeve* the prison/pub scene comprises a small but importantly placed section of the film, in *Anne Devlin* the site of the prison comprises a large portion of the film. Here the prison site is not peripheral; rather, it usurps the film's action and extricates the narrative from the traditional national history of Robert Emmet. The story of the 1803 uprising is generally the narrative of Emmet and his male comrades; if standard histories do mention Devlin at all, they cite her as the housekeeper who suffered in silence. In contradistinction to this culturally constructed version of history, Murphy makes Devlin the central character. Murphy recognized the significance of the prison for her film; in the press release/synopsis for *Anne Devlin*, Aeon Films Limited notes that the film reveals Devlin "as a woman of heroic stature whose voice, transcending its time and place in nineteenth century Ireland becomes the experience of all women who have endured imprisonment and torture for their beliefs." In this press release, the focus is on female incarceration as an experience many women would recognize.

In the trajectory of feminist film in Northern Ireland, *Anne Devlin* is distinct from *Maeve* not only because it renders the site of the prison more visible but also because it represents a woman who is incarcerated; for her role in the rebellion, Devlin was imprisoned from 1803 to 1806. Robert Emmet's unsuccessful 1803 rebellion occurred between Wolfe Tone's 1798 uprising and the Great Famine of 1845–47. Emmet, a Protestant from a wealthy family, planned to seize Dublin Castle, and on July 23, he led a small force into the streets of Dublin. The rebellion was poorly planned, and the small number of men was easily put down. Emmet and others were later captured. The rebellion emerged as agrarian fighting was at a zenith: Protestant yeoman and Irish landed gentry struggled to protect their property and power from secret Catholic societies that rebelled against the inequalities of the owner-tenant relationship and the penal laws that disallowed, among other things, land ownership.

*Anne Devlin* makes clear the specific class component of the uprising. Not only does the film highlight, as critics point out, Emmet's relationship with his wealthy girlfriend, Sarah Curran, but more important, the film indicates that Emmet's desire for a well-dressed military speaks of his distance from the class and gender concerns of the people. In one scene, after she has moved to Emmet's home at Butterfield Lane to act as his decoy-housekeeper, Anne sees the uniforms laid out for battle. Emmet, played by Bosco Hogan, emerges quietly behind her, and thinking that she is admiring the uniforms, he begins to discuss their beauty. Anne replies that "they look like a green version of the redcoats. We are ourselves. We should rebel as ourselves." Just as he fails to understand her reasons for participating in the rebellion, Emmet misunderstands Anne's comment about the uniform: "But Anne, it will be like a sea of green, like the sea itself rising up." "But the fighting will be in the streets," Anne insists, "how will the men get away?" Played by Brid Brennan, Anne is, of course, pointing out that Emmet's planning is faulty and his revolution merely an intellectual exercise. Yet when she makes a parallel between the British and Irish uniforms, Anne is also metaphorically suggesting that things will remain the same after the men march: unless there is an ideological change in addition to military action, Irish men will become merely a green version of the British. Audiences schooled in history and feminism may also read Anne's comment as an indication that life will remain substantially unchanged for women as well.

The class consciousness of the film is also exemplified with the character James Hope, played by Des McAleer. Based in Belfast, Hope and his family have traveled South to lend support to the rebellion; Hope is committed to the quest for class equality, which he supposes the revolution plans to make possible. However, after he speaks with Emmet and some of the other men, he recognizes that they are not planning for equality and also that they have not realistically assessed the needs of the mass population of Ireland. Emmet tells Hope and other men of his/the rebellion's plan to seize the Church of England. Hope is angered and insists that Emmet is not focusing on important sectarian and class concerns: "You can't expect the Protestant people of the North to risk everything for Catholic Emancipation. They need a guarantee that the whole structure will be changed. That all [private, church] property will be abolished." Emmet's failure to address class conflicts becomes obvious when he responds to Hope that "you knew right from the start that my strategy has been to emphasize what unites, what people are prepared to give rather than fragment the movement by bringing out our differences. What do you think ___ and Mr.___ would think if they heard you? All these attacks on property would alienate them and destroy us." Hope insists that "you're basing the revolution on the shopkeepers, not the working men. They'll be the first to hang you." Emmet fails to recognize the truth to this statement and notes that Hope is merely "insulting decent men who have put their faith in us." Hope's response to the phrase "decent men" reveals both his foresight and the failure of the uprising to speak to class concerns: "You mean your investors, the men who will run this country after we put the English out for them." Hope's words demonstrate not only how ill-conceived the revolution is but also the continuing difficulty of politics in the Republic and Northern Ireland today: there is little acknowledgment of the concerns of disparate groups of people. He recognizes that unless economic oppression and inequality are examined, the conditions that exist prerebellion will be present postrebellion.

Yet another little-explored component of the film is the class status of Anne's family, a status which is continually confronted through Anne's relation to imprisonment. Although Anne's social status is only hinted at in the film, in *The Anne Devlin Jail Journal*, compiled by Brother Luke Cullen from interviews with Anne Devlin, and itself the basis for Murphy's film, this status is made evident. In the preface to his manuscript, Cullen wrote the date 1857. He also noted that one of his last visits to Anne was in 1846; Anne died in 1851. Referring to Anne's covert position as the revolutionaries' decoy-housekeeper, Cullen begins his tale by describing Devlin as the "Co. Wicklow girl who was Robert Emmet's housekeeper" (9). In the chapter "A Rebel Family," Cullen notes that Devlin was born in 1780 to a farmer, Brian Devlin, who married a woman whose father was "a farmer in comfortable circumstances" (17). Anne reveals her mother's class status, a status interrupted both by her husband's tenant position and by the entire family's revolutionary activities: "Although my mother often spoke of the low and degraded state her family was reduced to from wealthy and respectable ancestry, yet she had no wish for commotion" (quoted on 38).

In the film, after Brian Devlin and his family have moved from the Darby farm and when his nephew, Arthur Devlin, and Robert Emmet request the family's assistance, Arthur Devlin remarks upon his uncle's prosperity: "Jesus you've done alright for yourself." The Devlin family is a relatively prosperous family, but because of the penal laws that prohibited Catholics from land ownership, they cannot own the farm. Still later in the tale, and also noted in Murphy's film, Anne is interrogated in jail on several occasions by a British soldier, Major Sirr, who questions her family's position: "What puzzles me is why a prosperous family like yours would get involved. Your father was in comfortable circumstances and it is not usual in this country for such persons to let their daughters go out in service." Sirr recognizes the class status of the family, one which would have made service unnecessary and even unthinkable (see Maria Luddy and Cliona Murphy, *Women Surviving*). To Sirr's feigned confusion regarding her status as a servant (he actually knows what her role in the rebellion was but wants her to confess), Anne replies that her father has a large family to support, and will not concede that her job was to act as a decoy to give the illusion that Butterfield Lane was a "real" home. Yet it is the status of home that Anne's place at Butterfield Lane invokes, because Butterfield Lane is *not* a home; it is a strategy center for the rebellion. The contradiction between the home and a strategy center foreshadows the links among the home, class status, and the prison.

When Anne arrives at Butterfield Lane, because she is a woman, Emmet's military men think of her as a housekeeper and not as a comrade in the rebellion. Upon her arrival, Emmet tells Anne that she is not really a servant, but moments later, one of his fellow military men, Thomas Russell, acts as if she is when he meets her in an upstairs corridor. "Who are you," he asks. "Anne Devlin, Sir," she replies. "Oh, well, fetch me some hot water, will you? And a dry towel as well, please." Certainly this scene indicates the class and gender inconsistencies within the rebellion. It also suggests that the contradiction between Anne's role as a real or pretend servant, along with the status of Butterfield Lane as a real or pretend home, runs parallel to the contradictions introduced into the Devlin home when it is contaminated by the presence of the state. As will be made clear later in this chapter, before the British soldiers come to the Devlin home, the house operates on relatively egalitarian principles. The relation between the Devlin home and the state finally ushers in and complicates the site of the prison.

In *The Anne Devlin Jail Journal,* Devlin speaks about her family's move to the house where they reside at the start of the uprising and notes that "our affairs were in a very prosperous way in the commencement of 1803" (quoted in Cullen, 30–32). Although theirs is a relatively prosperous home, after Anne leaves Butterfield Lane, and after she and other Catholics in the area are suspected of covert activity, the Devlin family home is searched first by unruly yeoman and then by the British authorities. This police search of the family home places Devlin's story not only in the midst of nationalist politics but also in the context of material concerns: specifically, police searches of the homes of political dissidents.

After she is tortured at Butterfield Lane by British authorities who are looking for Emmet, Anne returns home. Police arrive and take her and her family members to prison. In her interview with Cullen, Devlin describes this event, which the film reproduces— an event embedded in and perhaps continually reconstructed in her memory. Devlin's father reluctantly answers a knock at the door; the knock is that of a neighbor and the British authorities. As Devlin recalls: "My father still seemed reluctant, but he well knew that it would be forced open and he at last complied. As he unlocked the door he demanded their business and was arrested that moment. . . . we were scarcely allowed time to dress when we were hurried down to the lower part of the house. . . . we were now ready for marching. My mother was 50 years of age, my father something more, my elder sister 25, I was in my 24th year, and my next sister in her 22nd year. My brother Art was 20, John 18 and James 8 or 9" (quoted in Cullen, 53–54). Although Anne resists authority as much as she can by discreetly cutting the cord that has been tied around her father's hands, she and the other family members are marched off to prison, where Anne is arrested for treason and "treasonable practices."

In *Barred: Women, Resistance, and Political Detention,* Barbara Harlow speaks of the relationship between the home and the prison and insists on the significance of what she terms "the knock on the door": "Within the narrative of political detention, which is the attempted physical appropriation by the state of the political and personal identity of the detainee, the 'knock on the door' can be reconstructed as a political variant of the more blatant practice of 'house demolition'" (210). Although she is speaking specifically about Israel's current practice of demolishing Palestinian houses in the West Bank, Harlow underscores the effect of the knock-on-the-door scenario for other political prisoners and their families in diverse geographic locations.

In *Justice under Fire,* Jennings and his coauthors discuss not house demolitions but house searches in Northern Ireland. They argue that in the case of the latter, authorities' motivation is often to garner information and to encourage complicity. In the same book, Paddy Hillyard quotes from a text that details a soldier's report of a house search:

We did a search this morning. It was the house of a woman with five children. We went in about five thirty. Four of her kids had got measles and we had to tell her to get them up. We didn't wreck the house, but we turned it over properly, we did our job thoroughly. Her husband is a wanted man, and of course we didn't expect to find him there but we thought we might get some ammunition, or evidence he'd been there. On the whole she took it very well: she wasn't very pleased, but she didn't say much, just gave us dirty looks. I mean eight soldiers clumping round her house, and her and the kids standing there in their night clothes in the dark early hours getting cold. I'm surprised she didn't make more fuss: but perhaps she's getting used to it. After all, this is the thirteenth time she's had her house searched in three weeks. (quoted on 197–98)

This report testifies to the reasons for many house searches in Northern Ireland, as well as to the burden it places on women. As one might imagine, house searches are often imprinted in the memories of political detainees. In *Barred* Harlow indicates that many writings by prisoners not only recount this familiar event, the "knock on the door," but also convert it into an instance of political resistance and a space from which to reevaluate Western hegemonic narratives of the home, the individual, the family, and the significance of prison: "Political detention, while it can be sufficiently located within a configuration of ideological confrontations between what western literary historiography terms the individual and society, rearticulates the narrative of those confrontations instead as the state versus an organized political opposition. This symbolically overdetermined significance of 'home' and identity remains central to such conflicted narratives" (210–11). What Harlow means is that political detention, as detailed in literature (and, for my purposes, film), is often understood as a conflict between an individual and society. However, she argues that central to narratives of and about political detention are examinations of the meaning of "home" and "identity." Harlow reminds us that when we interpret detention, we must examine the home involved and analyze what the detention attempts to do to the stability of this home. In *Anne Devlin* political detention or even the threat of it disrupts a nationalist home.

In Murphy's film, then, the class contradictions in the Butterfield Lane home—contradictions which suggest the inconsistencies within the rebellion itself—introduce and prefigure the contradictions within the Devlin family home when the state uses the concept of home to disrupt resistant activity and to indicate the next step/site: the prison. In *Barred*, Harlow proceeds further and notes that "critical to the contested construction of home is the position a woman occupies in it, a position to which she may be confined as much by the resistance as by the state" (211). In the Devlin family home, imperialism intervenes to confine Anne and disrupt nationalist/familial egalitarianism. When Arthur Devlin notes to his uncle that "you've done alright for yourself," Brian Devlin insists that "we've worked hard. My wife runs a dairy and I let out the horses to the neighbors." Although Arthur implies that his uncle is responsible for this prosperity, Brian Devlin insists that the credit is due equally to him and his wife. When Arthur and Robert Emmet request the family's assistance, it is Winefred Devlin, Anne's mother, who has the final say, although the entire family discusses the proposal. Winefred Devlin not only notes that "no one in our family has ever gone out in service" but also questions the terms of the ultimate agreement: "You mean she's [Anne] not getting paid?" Finally, in *The Anne Devlin Jail Journal*, Anne recounts her mother's bravery in publicly handling the body of a man who was brutally executed. Readers and viewers can only see Winefred Devlin as an independent-minded women, one who makes decisions with her husband.

Although in the Devlin family home/knock-on-the-door scene we see the entire family (except for the youngest, a little girl accidentally left behind) marched off to jail, this is not Anne's first encounter with the prison site. Years earlier, when the family lived on the Darby estate, Brian Devlin was imprisoned. In the film, Devlin's visit to her father comprises one of the initial scenes, thus quickly establishing the significance of the prison to the narrative. It is unclear whether or not Brian Devlin is politically involved when he is initially imprisoned; nevertheless, he is incarcerated in Wicklow for two and a half years without being charged. According to Wicklow Jail rules, prisoners who have any means must support themselves. In the initial prison scenes, Anne brings food to her father and helps him wash. She will remain her father's caretaker while he is in prison.

In the first of these prison scenes, Brian Devlin is surprised to see his daughter, but she tells him that there has been trouble in the countryside and that "it's safer for a woman to travel these days." The two discuss what Brian Devlin terms the "madness" of Michael Dwyer, the rebel who remains in hiding in the Wicklow mountains and whose militant actions Brian Devlin insists "will have us all in here." Devlin also speaks of his fears that the authorities will use Anne to locate Dwyer, and finally Anne informs her father of local events, while suggesting how conscious she is of material circumstances:

**Anne: There's talk of their [landlords] putting out the small farmers and turning the estate into two or three big farms.**
**Brian: Mrs. Darby [Devlin's landlord] would never do that surely.**
**Anne: We haven't paid much rent these past two years.**

Brian Devlin naively assumes that the Darby landlords will not displace the small farmers, while Anne recognizes that because her father is in prison, the family has not been able to pay their rent; thus they may very well be evicted. Anne's fears are almost realized in the next scene; here Anne, her mother, and Mrs. Darby negotiate the terms under which the family may remain on the farm. The women contend with the very real material circumstance of trying to keep a roof over their head while Brian Devlin remains in jail. Understandably, he is concerned about his imprisonment, but he is also concerned about Dwyer. Anne's concern is with how the family will live.

On her next visit, Anne encourages her father to appeal his case.

He is reluctant to do so, however, for fear that he will be deported. Anne insists that if he were deported, the family would follow him. Finally, Brian Devlin urges his daughter to get away to Dublin "where these things don't happen." He correctly recognizes that much of the revolutionary activity is occurring on the land, in the country, but it is Anne who recognizes that the effects of such activity will be felt elsewhere: "You mean where you can't see them happening."

Anne Devlin's visit to her father only *partially* foreshadows her own incarceration; during her imprisonment, Anne will encounter peculiar challenges as a woman. In Harlow's *Barred* and in Pat Carlen's *Women's Imprisonment: A Study in Social Control,* the authors insist that the difficulties the state imposes on women in prison tend to be those associated with their gender and sex (women's bodies are censored and used differently than are men's); with their perceived relationship to family members (the idea of women's relation to children, parents, and spouses is used against them); and with women's perceived "femininity" (the construction of "femininity" is often used as a means to devise "appropriate" punishment for women). Incarceration is gendered, and when she is imprisoned, Anne is treated as a female prisoner. According to Frieda Kelly in *A History of Kilmainham Gaol: The Dismal House of Little Ease,* interrogators and wardens often treated female prisoners differently than they did males. Kelly also researches the actual Dr. Trevor (one of Anne's interrogators) and determines the doctor's distaste for all but one woman in his care.

Two of Anne's most sadistic interrogators in jail are Major Sirr and Dr. Trevor; both use Anne's family members, her sexuality, and her perceived femininity in an attempt to extort information from her. When a female warden helps Anne prepare for her first interrogation with Major Sirr, she tells her that she "must be strong. Don't let them break you." To this Anne responds with resignation, "Break what? They don't know what it is. There's nothing to break." Anne understands that while the male revolutionaries have not adequately understood her, these colonial authorities have even less of an idea of who she is or why she has participated in the rebellion. Yet Sirr assumes he does know Devlin, and he bases this assumption on preconceived notions of gender.

Major Sirr begins his interrogation by telling Anne all about the terrors of confinement, terrors which he maintains are harsh, "especially on a young woman" (66). Here Sirr insists that there are peculiar and especially harsh conditions with regard to women's imprisonment. Furthermore, although Major Sirr uses Anne's status as a woman, he speaks to her as though she is a disobedient child—a female child: "If you will be a good girl and will give what information you have about Mr. Emmet and his associates, we need not mention one word about your connection. . . . I will obtain £500 for you. You are a Catholic; you know what confession means and forgiveness." Anne responds that she has no information to suggest, and Sirr angrily remarks, "Don't be a fool; £500 is a handsome fortune. It's a fine dowry for a young woman." Sirr has already used Anne's family as a threat: first he lied to her and said that her family had surrendered, and then he told her that if she confessed, she could save her family. Now Sirr is asking Anne to betray her revolutionary activity and the activity of others, but he is making this request in terms specific to her status as a (marriageable) woman. Male prisoners, of course, would not have been offered a dowry in exchange for information; Sirr makes it obvious that he views Anne as a woman and will thus become completely exasperated when she does not behave as he thinks a woman should. Because she confounds his sense of how a woman should behave and think, Anne will be punished more unusually than will many of the men who participated in the rebellion. She is imprisoned longer than the others, and Sirr tries to "break" her differently.

When Anne remains obstinate in her refusal to discuss the rebellion or the people involved, Sirr seethes with anger: "You are the most desperate young woman I've ever come across, and I'll keep you in jail all the days of your life as a warning to women like you." Sirr wants to use Anne as an example not merely of punishable "criminal" behavior, but also, more serious to him, of behavior punishable *because* it is exhibited by a woman. It is not just that

Anne has transgressed the boundaries of "acceptable behavior/criminal behavior," but, more important, that she has transgressed colonial gender boundaries. As a colonized woman, she should be both docile and passive. In *In Other Worlds: Essays in Cultural Politics,* Gayatri Spivak argues that according to an imperialist mentality, colonial women can be subservient and oppressed; they can also be judged by the standards of white femininity, but they should not appear strong, independent, or steadfast in their cultural ways and mores.

Earlier, at her tribunal (a tribunal conducted by Sirr and one other officer), Sirr notes that Anne is "dead to the noble feelings that adorn the character of a woman" and states that she "will hang for it." Sirr does not say that Anne will hang for her "crime" of treason; rather, she will be hanged because she has failed to conform to *his* and colonial expectations of what a woman should be. This is presumably the most serious crime of all. Also, because she has transgressed the boundaries of femininity, Anne is housed on the male side of the prison and is thus desexed by her male jailers. Murphy consciously avoids detailing physical torture to concentrate on the psychological violence that is inflicted upon Anne. While she does this to focus on the gendered nature of Anne's imprisonment, by avoiding scenes of torture, Murphy is also making a statement about how the media portrays conflict in Northern Ireland. Furthermore, she refuses to be complicit in patriarchal cinema that depicts violence against women and thus contributes to audience voyeurism (1994).

As we have seen, according to Barbara Harlow and Pat Carlen, the peculiar difficulties female prisoners encounter in jail and under interrogation stem in part from preconceived notions of "femininity." Carlen studies, among other areas, the method of discipline in the Scottish women's prison, Cornton Vale; she insists that "familiness ['woman as situated within a prescribed family structure'] is one dominant conceptual axis along which women's imprisonment is conceived by the Scottish judicial and penal authorities. Femininity is another" (103). She continues, "Together with the insistence that deviant women should be interpolated as members of a family and reconstructed as lifelong candidates for domesticity, is the insistence that because prisoners in Cornton Vale are treated as women, they should behave accordingly" (103). In *Anne Devlin*, Major Sirr relies both on prescribed notions of femininity and on the concept of the family in an attempt to extort information from Anne. As a result, Anne's determination not to reveal her knowledge of the revolution is less a demonstration of the subversive potential of female silence (as one critic would have it) and more a resolve not to participate in colonial constructions of gender.

Perhaps Anne's most perverse interrogator, however, is Dr. Trevor, inspector of prisons and superintendent of Kilmainham Jail, where Major Sirr has her transferred. Although Dr. Trevor maltreats her, denies her medical care, and is responsible for her brother's death, Anne still refuses to provide information. Trevor displays his exasperation: "I've only seen one woman hanged, Devlin, and I'd not like to see another, and yet, I'd travel any distance to see you hanged. I'd feel pleasure in pulling the rope." On another occasion, he describes Anne as the "female state prisoner," highlighting her gendered status. Later, when the state is exonerating all prisoners at Kilmainham, Dr. Trevor moves Anne to a different prison, so she will not be freed. When he comes to tell her this news, Dr. Trevor caresses Anne's hair and face, indicating not only that he can and will touch her whenever he so desires, but also that he can and may do so in a sexual manner.

The Kilmainham Jail section of the film also examines the extent to which class structures in Ireland remain intact during incarceration. Dr. Trevor visits the makeshift cafeteria for the (male) prisoners and tells them that their complaints about the lack of food have been reviewed. He remarks that "the government has decided that prisoners should be classified according to their station in life. Therefore, gentlemen prisoners should have meat and wine, and peasants and mechanics will eat in the manner they're used to." There is a moment of silence from the revolutionaries who fought in Emmet's uprising. After this short moment, however, one of the men takes his seat at the table reserved for those who would be classified as former gentlemen, thus indicating that the rebellion has never been about class concerns.

In 1806, with the help of the jailer's wife, Anne is finally released from Kilmainham. Now in very poor physical health and destitute, she visits her family home and remains there for some time. She eventually marries, has one child, becomes a washerwoman, and dies in poverty and obscurity. Pat Murphy's film does not feature Anne's death or even her life after prison; it concludes with Devlin's release from prison. In this way, Murphy focuses not on the rebellion itself but rather on the particular effects of this conflict upon women, especially upon one woman who was imprisoned. *Anne Devlin* is significant not only because of this focus but also because it is the second film released by a woman that explores incarceration and connects it with gender and class. Yet *Anne Devlin* also suggests implications for the Republic and Northern Ireland in more contemporary times; like Devlin, who worked for the nationalist cause but was viewed merely as a handmaiden during and after the revolution, some (Republican) women today could find themselves relegated to male preconceptions of a different Northern Ireland.

Finally, *Anne Devlin* makes an important point about material conditions that will be taken up by other filmmakers. When the film portrays Devlin in the typical pietà of the Madonna and child or the Mother Ireland image, it does so with a difference. First, Devlin is holding her dying brother, not her son. Also, this young boy is not dying as a martyr or savior; rather, he is dying as a result of material conditions: he is dying of malnutrition and lack of medical treatment. Second, Devlin has by now stopped menstruating. She is definitely not a mother. Thus, through cinema, Murphy asserts the inefficacy of the image of Mother Ireland for Devlin as well as for contemporary women.

Other female filmmakers continue to explore women's specific relationship to nationalism and the Mother Ireland icon, but they too insist upon the primacy of material conditions. For them, material concerns are those conditions that are publicly discussed in the Republic and Northern Ireland in the 1980s and 1990s. The conditions include reproductive freedom, censorship, the women's movement, and incarceration.

# Feminist Film after Pat Murphy: *Mother Ireland,* *Hush-A-Bye Baby,* and *The Visit*

If this [pregnancy] is a problem for people they'll have to deal with it. The same with Sean. I stood by him through it all: the blanket, the dirt and the deaths. Now I'll see if he's got the strength to stand by me.

(Orla Walsh, *The Visit*, 1992)

Sinn Fein is opposed to the attitudes and forces in society that compel women to have abortions, and which criminalises those who do. We accept the need for abortion where a woman's life is at risk or grave danger (e.g., all forms of cancer) and in cases of rape or child sexual abuse.

(Sinn Fein, *Sinn Fein Women's Policy Document*, 1992)

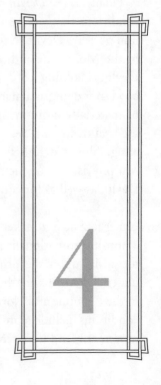

LIKE PAT MURPHY, who is considered Ireland's foremost feminist filmmaker, many other feminists have made films that look at women's relation to gender, nationalism, and incarceration. Anne Crilly's documentary *Mother Ireland* (1988) examines the tensions among nationalism, feminism, and Republicanism and makes comparisons to the suffragette movement. For my purposes, the film becomes most significant in its exploration of three female prisoners—two who see their role as a support base for male Republicans, and one who begins to question this leadership but only by indicating that the fault lies with society, not Republicanism. In Margo Harkin's *Hush-A- Bye Baby* (1989), Gorretti, a Catholic teenager from Derry's Bogside, the working-class area that was the site of the civil rights marches in 1968 and 1969 and "Bloody Sunday" in 1972, becomes pregnant. Gorretti's predicament is exacerbated by the loss of her boyfriend: at the same time she discovers she is pregnant, he is taken into custody by the Royal Ulster Constabulary (RUC). Furthermore, at one point, Gorretti walks past the by-now-famous "You are now entering the free Derry" wall. This wall commemorates the civil rights marches, and the film implicitly asks, freedom for whom? Finally, in Orla Walsh's *The Visit* (1992), Sheila Molloy becomes pregnant while her husband is serving a long-term sentence in Belfast's the Maze: Her Majesty's Prison at Long Kesh, the jail which holds many of the North's political dissidents. When her lover learns of her condition, he asks Sheila to run away with him to Dublin, where he can obtain employment. To this Sheila responds, "This whole thing [the affair, the pregnancy] was not about you or him [her husband]. It was about me. Everything has always been decided for me; now I'm going to have a life for myself." Whether they explore teenage pregnancy or women's position within Republicanism, these filmmakers highlight the prison as the site where women's material conditions are made obvious.

Mother Ireland

As though to indicate that her film is informed by Murphy's questioning of women and historical narratives, Anne Crilly's *Mother Ireland* specifically invokes the site of the prison to suggest women's continual oppression vis-à-vis state and nationalist forces. The film hints that women who have fought and have been incarcerated for the nationalist cause may later be disappointed by this cause. While in Crilly's film the material effects of incarceration (including footage of a hunger strike) are emphasized, the fact that the film itself has been censored forces us to consider material considerations of filmmaking as well.

The 1988 documentary *Mother Ireland* was directed by Anne Crilly and produced by Derry Film and Video under a remit by Channel 4 to showcase "underrepresented groups" (Crilly 1994). Under the workshop declaration of the British film union ACTT in 1981, and in agreement with the British Film Institute, Channel 4, the Regional Arts Associations, and the Independent Film and Video Association, a nonprofit cooperative that meets specific regulations may be eligible for a remit (Emerman, 40). Derry Film and Video fitted the guidelines. Prior to *Mother Ireland*, the group produced *Derry Video News,* a news program; *Strip-searching: Security or Subjugation,* an examination of the strip-search policy of Northern Ireland's women's prison; and *Planning,* an exploration of military involvement in Northern Ireland city planning.

In the words of its director, *Mother Ireland* explores "how Ireland is portrayed as a woman in Irish culture and how this image developed as a nationalist motif" (1991, 163). Some of the women interviewed who explore this image include Bernadette Devlin McAliskey, former MP and civil rights activist; Pat Murphy, filmmaker; Rita O'Hare, former director of Sinn Fein Women's Department and editor of *Republican News*; Mairead Farrell, former political prisoner and member of the IRA; and members of Cumann na mBan, the now-defunct Republican women's auxiliary organization dating back to the beginning of the century. Crilly notes that the film "also examines how nationalist and republican women, the daughters who fought for Mother Ireland, relate to this image and whether it has any relevance today" (163). Finally, Crilly makes clear that the argument between feminism and Republicanism is one prefigured at the turn of the century by differences between the suffragettes and Republicans.

Although *Mother Ireland* has been presented to small audiences, conferences, and university groups, it holds the dubious distinction of being the first film banned under the 1988 Hurd Ban and, as such, could not initially be shown on television and was not screened in public theaters. One woman interviewed in the film, Mairead Farrell, was shot and killed by Britain's special forces on March 6, 1988, just one week after the film was sent to Channel 4 for final editing. While the film was held in wait during the inquest regarding the shooting of Farrell and her companions, the Hurd Ban (named for then home secretary Douglas Hurd), which placed broadcast restrictions on members of specified political organizations, was introduced. According to Crilly in "Banning History," the legal department at Channel 4 encouraged the broadcast of *Mother Ireland,* but in mid-October, Derry Film and Video was asked to make another cut: to remove Farrell's interview. Once the Hurd Ban went into effect on October 19, 1988, that cut was no longer optional: the ban disallowed the broadcast of five interviews in the film, one of which was Farrell's.

Even before the ban, however, Channel 4 requested the following deletions from the film: the Christy Moore song "Unfinished Revolution," an extract from an Italian television program that featured masked female IRA members carrying out arm drills, a few shots of masked Cumann na mBan women, a nationalist poster (which was on the wall behind Farrell as she was interviewed), and an entire sequence of new footage of plastic bullet victim Emma Groves, just after she had been blinded. Derry Film and Video agreed to make these cuts, but they became unnecessary after the Hurd Ban; the film could not be released even with the cuts. In a revision of section 29 of the Broadcasting Act, this new legislation required broadcasters to refrain not only from airing direct statements from representatives of specific organizations

(UDA [Ulster Defence Association], UVF [Ulster Volunteer Force], IRA, Sinn Fein) but also from airing any words "which support or invite support for these organizations." This new ruling could cover almost any person whose words were deemed inappropriate and also restricted archival footage. In the Republic of Ireland, section 31 (in place since 1960) censored *Mother Ireland* as well. In 1994, section 31 was revoked, however.

In addition to *Mother Ireland's* plight as a censored film, the film is significant because it highlights the issue of female incarceration. Two of the Cumann na mBan women interviewed were imprisoned—one was interned twice, once after the Easter Rising and once again in the 1970s with her daughter; another was imprisoned and went on a hunger strike after the Easter Rising—as was Mairead Farrell. Eighteen months before she was killed, Farrell was released after having served ten years in Armagh Prison, where she had been sentenced for planting bombs. She was classified as a criminal at Armagh, and Farrell and others participated in a no-wash strike and a hunger strike; they did this in sympathy with the male hunger strikers and for their own benefit.

In *Mother Ireland,* although Farrell stops just short of critiquing males within the Republican movement, she expressly denies the usefulness of the concept of Mother Ireland for women. She almost criticizes Republican men when she states that male Republican prisoners did not understand that the female strikers were not only supporting the men but also protesting for themselves. Yet Farrell does not quite criticize male Republicans; instead she notes that their attitude was merely a reflection of "society at large." She denies the usefulness of the concept of Mother Ireland when she says that while they were in prison, Farrell and other women would state, "Mother Ireland get off our backs." In my interview with Anne Crilly, she notes that Farrell's vehement denial of the usefulness of the Mother Ireland icon is especially interesting when we recognize that Farrell died thinking that she was defending Ireland (1994). Importantly, in the documentary, Farrell explains why she became involved in the Republican movement; she makes explicit the connections between internment or incarceration and female politicization: "Living on the Falls Road, I saw internment, I saw the British soldiers. . . . I just got a political education from looking around me." Farrell expressly links her own political involvement to internment; she became political in part because she saw people around her interned.

Like *Maeve*, *Mother Ireland* does not feature the site of the prison, except through archival footage that features a female hunger striker after the Easter Rising, but the specter of the prison is indicated by the three women mentioned above, and especially by the context surrounding Farrell, her incarceration, and her murder by Britain's special forces.

When Mairead Farrell mentions the no-wash strike, feminists from the Republic and Northern Ireland must certainly be aware of the controversy that this strike generated within women's movements. In *Against the Grain: The Contemporary Women's Movement in Northern Ireland*, Eileen Evason notes that although there have always been issues that have divided the women's movement in the North—issues as diverse as class differences, reproductive rights, political tension and/or sectarianism, and "the corrosive and demoralising effect of Thatcherism" (15)—one particularly destabilizing division occurred surrounding the Armagh dirt strike. Evason discusses political protests and the Armagh strike in particular:

In 1980 women in Armagh prison joined the "no wash" protest and three went on hunger strike. These events brought differences which had simmered in the NIWRM [Northern Ireland Women's Rights Movement] since its early days to a boiling point. The demand that all women's groups should come out in support of the Armagh women produced bitterness and tension. Many women's groups simply refused to take a position and there was never any prospect of unity on this issue. Some, whilst wishing to give support to the Armagh women, did not wish to give general support to the republican movement and felt they were not being given the space to make this distinction. Some were in favour of Special Category status on humanitarian grounds and were appalled at the suffering that occurred. At the same time they could not accept the assumption that they had a duty to give support by virtue of their feminism. (19)

Evason's words indicate that the Armagh strike foregrounded the tension between feminism and nationalism and the difficulty of creating a women's movement in a (post)colonial site.

In "Women on the Margin: The Women's Movement in Northern Ireland, 1973–1988," Carmel Roulston analyzes the women's movement in the North and distinguishes it from other modern feminist coalitions: "Divisions among feminists over politics and ideology are a recurrent feature of all modern women's movements; in Northern Ireland, the familiar socialist/revolutionary feminist camps are fragmented even further by differences over Republicanism and the IRA campaign. It is difficult even to set out the problem, as there is a lack of consensus over what it is" (219). Roulston states, for example, that the Belfast Women's Collective, replacing the Socialist Women's Group, was finally dissolved when the "tension between republicanism/nationalism and feminism became particularly acute for feminists during the period of the campaign for political status for prisoners of terrorist offenses" (228). Although the group initially supported the protests by the women in Armagh, they eventually became divided over the way the campaign (of assistance) was handled; thus their dissolution became complete.

The Armagh strike also reached popular consciousness as feminists in the North and South publicly discussed the issue and the women's movement's response to it. In "It Is My Belief That Armagh Is a Feminist Issue," McCafferty insists that Armagh is a feminist issue because it is about "bodily integrity" (1994, 20). Although in "The Women's Movement in the Republic of Ireland, 1970–1990," Ailbhe Smyth does not mention the Armagh protest specifically, she does note that one of the early contemporary collectives, the Irish Women's Liberation Movement, entered into a heated debate over housing issues in 1971. Smyth maintains that this was actually a debate about ideological differences between those who wished to concern themselves with "specific women's issues as opposed to social issues" (1993, quoted on 254). In other words, the IWLM discussed whether or not material issues were feminist issues. Smyth notes that underneath this debate simmered different tensions than the ones voiced: "One senses the shadow of republicanism—always present, but rarely allowed to surface directly and explicitly" (1993, 255). Women in the Republic and Northern Ireland force a reconsideration of what difference within the women's movement can mean in a (post)colonial site. Read in this context, *Mother Ireland* complicates nationalist narratives by shifting cinema from a focus on nationalism to an emphasis on material conditions such as the women's movement, bodily integrity, and the division between nationalism and feminism.

Given its limited showings, *Mother Ireland* was generally well received. However, although she is not speaking only about *Mother Ireland,* in "Beyond Women in Green: Some Remarks on Irish Feminist Film," Kathleen Nutt argues for a feminist cinema "beyond green yes, but for all that not orange either" (13). She states that in order to subvert the history of the "Irish rebel" on screen, more attention needs to be given to "outsiders" such as RUC officers or victims of the IRA. Finally, Nutt proposes a feminist film that examines "the ways in which many women faced with common problems . . . have managed to suspend political difference and organize themselves for social justice" (13). Nutt insists that, to date, feminist filmmakers in Ireland have participated in the film industry according to the dominant narrative of nationalist struggle; she also maintains that the "historical and ideological connections between feminism and anti-Unionism" (11) are significant in this regard. Her argument is provocative, but Nutt could proceed farther to acknowledge the ways in which feminist filmmakers have complicated the nationalist narrative. With a few notable exceptions, I would agree that feminist cinema in and/or about Northern Ireland in the 1980s and early 1990s has been dominated by nationalist concerns or by a critique of nationalism. However, the reasons for this are actually much more complex than Nutt contends because they are tied up with how and why women have learned to speak out in various communities. Perhaps because of their early participation in nationalism, nationalist women have literally had more practice "speaking up" and getting thier message across. Finally, what has been termed the "common problems" approach to Northern Ireland has received critical attention elsewhere and could perhaps both be complicated by and also complicate Nutt's argument (see Foster [1991], Bell, and Coulter [1993]). Crilly herself also has much to offer regarding the need for diverse voices in film.

According to Crilly, *Mother Ireland*'s objective was to allow for the voice of women for whom the icon of Mother Ireland resonates; Crilly insists that if the film recognizes nationalist women, this is because of her particular background. Also, Crilly is especially self-conscious about her role as a filmmaker (1994). In fact, when I spoke with her, Crilly noted that as a documentary filmmaker, she had helped to construct audience perceptions of Mairead Farrell, for example, by placing a nationalist poster above Farrell during her on-screen interview (1994). Crilly recognizes how she shaped the documentary form of her film, and her thinking on the subject could productively inform film studies in the Republic and Northern Ireland.

### Hush-A-Bye Baby

Although the controversy surrounding *Mother Ireland* continued, Derry Film and Video still received funding for a while, and in 1989, under the direction of Margo Harkin, the workshop produced *Hush-A-Bye Baby*. Harkin and Stephanie English cowrote the screenplay. Harkin explicitly conceived of *Hush-A-Bye Baby* as a feature that would digress from the "realism" of documentary; however, she still wanted to place the film in the "real" city of Derry and to focus on contemporary issues for women. In so doing, Harkin created a film that explores many of the same issues as the previous cinema I have discussed. *Hush-A-Bye Baby* did not have to contend with the concerns that faced *Mother Ireland,* but, according to Harkin, the film was censored by some. When she wrote to the Hall Cinema in Derry, a small theater run by the local Catholic Church, she was told that *Hush-A-Bye Baby* would not be screened because of its "unsympathetic spiritual treatment," which the priest of the church feared would render the film a commercial failure (Harkin 1991, 115). Though it was shown on television, when Harkin spoke about the film in 1991, it had not been released in the Hall Cinema (115). The film did provoke controversy, particularly among those Harkin identifies as the "right wing" contingent of the Republican movement (134); nevertheless, it was a commercially successful venture.

Although Harkin recognizes the significance of her film being censored by a church and the importance of showing it in theaters, *Hush-A-Bye Baby* was funded largely by television broadcasters (Channel 4 and RTE). Harkin has spoken of the fact that she wanted to reach a television audience, an audience that may or may not have previous knowledge but could learn by simply "tuning in" (Sullivan 1998). While there are, of course, various distinctions between television and film, it is significant that *Hush-A-Bye Baby* represents a very different television broadcast of the troubles, one that refuses to see the national conflict as the only or even the primary event in a young woman's life. Rather, nationalism is imbricated in other material conditions.

*Hush-A-Bye Baby* explores a young teenage woman's experience in the Bogside, a contemporary working-class community in Derry, Northern Ireland. The Bogside is usually remembered as the site of the civil rights marches of 1968 and 1969 and "Bloody Sunday" in 1972. Goretti, played by Emer McCourt, is a Catholic girl who becomes pregnant. The film responds to cultural debates on the island concerning the divorce referendum, reproductive freedom, and a young women's sexual, political, and economic freedom in Derry. When Goretti discovers she is pregnant, her boyfriend, Ciaran, who is played by Michael Liebmann, is taken into police custody; therefore, the film acknowledges that sexual, religious, and economic freedom for some in Northern Ireland is often complicated by women's relation to the state through the prison. Yet while Goretti's boyfriend represents nationalist and Republican communities in the North, the film is more concerned with exploring Goretti's material conditions and acknowledging that incarceration is but one of these conditions.

Although the prison becomes a crucial site in the film, *Hush-A-Bye Baby*'s most dominant image is the cultural icon the Virgin Mary. In an interview with Patsy Murphy, Margo Harkin says that before she conceived of the film linguistically, she saw it in images, and the most dominant was "very over the top": it was the image of a pregnant Virgin Mary (1990, 9). From the beginning of the film, this image is invoked. In initial scenes, a priest explains the concept of marriage to teenage girls. As he speaks of the sacrament, a statue of the Blessed Mary looms over him. One of the protagonist's friends is played by Sinead O'Conner; she dresses herself in rosaries, a veil, and white gloves in the privacy of her bedroom, while Goretti, her sister, and her sister's children light candles in homage to Mary as verses of the hymn "Ava Maria" echo behind them. In the final scene of the film, Goretti, who has yet to tell her family she is pregnant, appears to go into labor while she is in bed. Before she awakens, Goretti dreams of statues of Mary. The images are fragmented: at first she sees Mary's face, then her stomach, then the statue's eye becomes a human eye. Finally, the face takes on the guise of a human. As intriguing as this dream sequence is, perhaps the most compelling scene occurs when Goretti and her friend Dinky visit the Gaeltacht (Irish-speaking region) in Donegal. At one point, Goretti and Dinky walk past a grotto, and, without hesitation, the two stop to pray. Later, after Goretti has told Dinky that she is pregnant, not only do the two walk past the grotto without stopping, but Dinky commands it sternly, but also with humor, "You better not fucking move."

Studies as diverse as Marina Warner's *Alone of All Her Sex: The Myth and Cult of the Virgin Mary* and Julia Kristeva's "Stabat Mater" have examined the iconography of the Virgin. However, this icon takes on a particular significance within the context of contemporary Ireland. In February of 1983, in Kerry, Ireland, there was a report of a moving statue of the Virgin Mary; during that year, sightings were reported throughout the Republic. In "Virgin on the Rocks" in *Seeing Is Believing: Moving Statues in Ireland,* Nell McCafferty suggests that the phenomenon of the moving statue is a direct result of Ireland's highly publicized debates surrounding female sexuality, divorce, and abortion. For many, the Virgin is a site of stability in these times; according to McCafferty, "The Blessed Virgin does not mention sex. She walks right away from it. She is adored" (McCafferty 1985, 58). Yet for women, as is indicated in Harkin's film, the image of the virgin is not one of stability.

According to Harkin, the importance of religion and sexual oppression are becoming increasingly complex and are replacing what was formerly a cinematic emphasis on nationalism. In the trajectory of films this book has analyzed thus far, Harkin's is the least overtly concerned with nationalism. Goretti's predicament is informed by the Catholic and nationalist mores she has internalized; however, Harkin extricates her plight even farther from Pat Murphy's protagonist's ideological argument between feminism and nationalism to center on a young woman's daily material issues. Although *Hush-A-Bye Baby* could discuss solely or mostly the issue of nationalism (because it takes place in Derry's Bogside), the film suggests instead that nationalism is merely one ideology that participates in the construction of a young woman.

*Hush-A-Bye Baby* is set in Northern Ireland in 1984, and the debates surrounding issues such as the moving statues, as well as the divorce and abortion referendums in the Republic, are signaled in it. When Goretti is studying Irish in the Gaeltacht, she is baking a cake and hears a radio broadcast about the abortion referendum. In 1983 women and men in the Republic voted to "defend the lives of the unborn"; although women's groups, some members of the labor party, and a substantial group of citizens had supported the abortion referendum, religious, conservative, and some political groups lobbied against it. Ostensibly at issue was the 1861 Offenses Against the Person Act, the British law that not only outlaws abortion but is also used against political dissidents. When the Republic put forward its own constitution in 1937, it left this act unaltered. After the 1983 referendum, the Eighth Amendment to the constitution was added; it mandated the following: "The state acknowledges the right to life of the unborn, and, with due regard to the equal right to life of the mother, guarantees in its laws to respect, and as far as practicable by its laws to defend and vindicate that right" (*Constitution, Republic of Ireland,* article 40.3.3).

This amendment not only prohibits abortion but also uses the rhetoric of "motherhood" to suggest how the law views women; the constitutional amendment refers not to women but to mothers. Legally, then, with reference to a fetus, a woman is a mother first and will be judged in terms of the social mores of domesticity.

In 1986, perhaps still reeling from the controversy of 1983, the Republic of Ireland voted down the divorce referendum as well but ultimately made marriage dissolution legal in 1996. Although it was guaranteed later in Northern Ireland than it was in Britain, divorce is legal in the North. Contraception is more readily available in the North, although it is now legal in the Republic as well. Abortion has not been legalized in Northern Ireland, but women do have the right to travel for a termination of pregnancy. Because of the North's more permissive legislation and because Catholic opinion is in the minority, many believe that Northern Ireland is more liberal in its religious/cultural attitudes. Yet this is not always the case. According to feminists, "Both Protestant and Catholic churches have conservative views on women's position. It is often believed that the north (in relation to the south) represents a liberal haven where women have unlimited access to contraception, but this legalistic reality disguises the pressures exerted upon women by religion. . . . the absence of any veneration of Mary on the Protestant side does not mean that Protestant women are any better off because Protestantism, particularly the Calvinist brand so pervasive in the north, is a patriarchal religion where the image of women is invisible" (Ward and McGivern 1980).

With reference to the particular context of Derry, Northern Ireland, both Bernadette Devlin McAliskey and Margaret Ward have offered their observations. In *Mother Ireland* McAliskey speaks of the inconsistencies within nationalist politics and notes that all the "internal contradictions" that were present in Derry pre-1969 are present post-1969: "Derry wasn't that free this side [that is, women's side, a pointed reference to the barricades that were erected in 1969] of the wall"; "Derry women were still making three square meals a day, and Derry men were still eating them." Ward states that after 1969, although street committees were formed to control defense and social welfare, women, who had long been the breadwinners in many Derry families, were ignored (Ward and McGivern 1980, 579–85). When the pregnant Goretti walks by the "You are now entering the free Derry" wall, the film signals these inconsistencies. Post-1969 and another generation later, as a woman, Goretti is still trapped by the same circumstances that would have oppressed her earlier: sexuality, religion, class, and state intervention.

Yet Goretti's pregnancy and her friend's dictum that the statue better not "fucking move" are also related to what in Ireland became known as the Kerry Babies Case and the case of Ann Lovett. Each of these demonstrated Ireland's ambivalence about and hostility toward female sexuality and reproductive choice. In 1983 the Kerry Babies inquiry was formed to investigate how police could have suspected Joanne Hayes of a crime she did not commit, the murder of a baby found miles from her home. Hayes's own baby died in childbirth, and when another baby was found dead in County Kerry, both Hayes's priest and a local hospital alerted authorities and suggested her culpability. When police and psychologists questioned Hayes, they noted that she did not display a "sufficient degree of guilt" regarding the death of her baby and therefore deduced that she may have conceived twins, killed them both, and buried one miles away. Although the inquest was established to rectify this absurdity, the judges present pursued a line of questioning similar to that of the police.

Ann Lovett was a fifteen-year-old girl who died after giving birth next to the grotto of the Virgin Mary in County Westmeath in January of 1984. Her baby also died, and her fourteen-year-old sister later committed suicide.

Finally, although it occurred after Harkin's film was produced, *Hush-A-Bye Baby* should be read in the context of the notorious 1992 X Case. In the Republic, the X Case caused notoriety because a fourteen-year-old who had been raped was initially denied access to travel to England for an abortion. The parents of the young girl reported the alleged rape to the police and questioned the feasibility of securing tissue from the fetus as evidence against the rapist. The police then barred the girl and her family from traveling, and although the girl was suicidal, the court initially determined that the health of the "baby" was more important than that of the "mother." She had to remain in Ireland. Finally, amid public outcry and a ruling by the Supreme Court, the girl was permitted to leave the country and presumably did go to England for an abortion. The Supreme Court overturned the original ruling because her psychological state was in jeopardy; detaining her would pose a risk to her right to life. Though the girl was allowed to travel, the court's ruling does not assist women, because it can be used to detain women to keep them from going abroad. In interviews and published discussions, Margo Harkin has stated that the film should be read in the context of these events. Goretti's interest in the radio broadcast refers to these cultural connections, as does her friend's comment to the statue.

Although these events are important to people in the North, they occurred in the Republic. Yet the film also illustrates that Goretti's predicament is made even more complex by the specificities of daily life in Northern Ireland. Not long after Goretti discovers she is pregnant, her boyfriend, Ciaran, is remanded by the RUC. His imprisonment illustrates how through incarceration, the state can affect the life of a young woman.

From the moment when Goretti and Ciaran meet in Irish language class through his incarceration, the usefulness of the Irish language, long considered a tool for nationalism, is questioned by Harkin. Once, after a date, Ciaran and Goretti are stopped by the border patrol, and Ciaran speaks in Irish. Surprisingly, the soldier not only responds in Irish but also speaks it more fluently than does Ciaran. The officer does not detain Ciaran, but their brief encounter encourages an examination of what some nationalists and Republicans think is the subversive potential of the Irish language.

After colonization and the imposition of the penal laws, the Irish language was outlawed. Irish was therefore spoken clandestinely, and to speak it was to resist colonial authority. Later, Irish prisoners used the language to communicate with one another, and today there has been a renewed interest in the language as some struggle to more clearly define what they view as their Irish identity. Yet Harkin's film reveals that one's use of the Irish language does not demonstrate one's identity; indeed identity not only is a shifting category but also is not *necessarily* defined by language. Furthermore, Ciaran cannot use Irish as a subversive method of communication because the state has already appropriated it; the state speaks it more fluently than does the nationalist!

The film juxtaposes the Irish language's uselessness for the nationalist and/or the Republican movement with the language's uselessness for a woman. With an Irish dictionary by her side, Goretti struggles to compose a letter to Ciaran. When she realizes that she does not know the Irish word for "pregnant," she tries to look it up and then realizes that there is no such word. In Irish, one must say/write "carrying a family/a giompas." Though many nationalists hail its emancipatory possibilities, in this instance, the Irish language is a constraining force for a girl. And while the Irish language is assumed to connote a specific Irish identity, a pregnant woman is only identified in terms of her status as a mother. Goretti's difficulty in finding the words to indicate her pregnant status parallels her difficulty in speaking of her pregnancy to an incarcerated Ciaran.

Whereas the Irish language and, by association, Republicanism neglect the individual woman with respect to pregnancy, the state disallows her words altogether and therefore also fails to recognize her status. Ultimately, Goretti writes Ciaran in Irish and informs him of her pregnancy. However, he never receives the letter. Not only are all letters to prisoners censored, but in Northern Ireland, letters written in Irish are confiscated. Barbara Harlow reminds us that because prison letters are censored, when they appear within a prison narrative, critical theorists must read these cultural documents for how they signal the relation between literary genres and material conditions. For Harlow, restrictions such as censorship and frequency and length of letters "present a dramatic example of the necessary connections between the formal criteria of genre and historical and institutional circumstances" (21). Thus Goretti's letter to Ciaran should be read for the way it is used by the state and for its uselessness for Goretti herself: the letter is censored by the state and further distances her from Ciaran.

The trope of the prison letter further suggests the particular significance of information gathering in Northern Ireland. Because England has long applied its method of governing the colonies to Northern Ireland, the state has placed a primary importance on the gathering of information about suspected political dissidents. "When the army entered Northern Ireland in 1969, it introduced a new policing technique based on its experience in the colonies. The foundation of its approach was the belief in the importance of intelligence" (Jennings et al., 194). The approach to information gathering is as follows: "The centerpiece of the army system was a card personality index. This noted the details of all 'suspected subversives' in each unit's operating area. Each card obtained information not only on the individual but on other family members and included religion, occupation, car details and lists of associates. These cards were cross-referenced to house cards and to a number of other cards indeces [sic] including those for vehicle records" (Jennings et al., 194).

Yet with advances in technology and because of tension between the police and army regarding "access to information," information gathering has become more sophisticated: "The RUC now has one of the largest computer installations of any police force in Europe. It has developed four main systems: a Command and Control system, which at present is available only in the Belfast area but is to be extended; a Criminal Information Retrieval (CIR) system, and a Data Reference Centre concerned primarily with the coalition and analysis of the terrorist use of firearms" (Jennings et al., 195). The RUC's emphasis upon data collection (an emphasis that extends to confiscating letters written in Irish) allows it to have information about Goretti and to prevent her from passing it along to her boyfriend.

Ciaran's incarceration is significant in other ways, however. Although we do not actually see much of his character, Ciaran is constructed as a young male teenager for whom life in Derry is fraught with tension. After Goretti and Ciaran's first date, Ciaran skips home whistling. As he turns a corner, he is stopped by the border patrol, and immediately his demeanor changes. The state imposes its domination on teenage romance. Harkin has said that Ciaran is a figure "on the fringes of Republicanism," which can mean that he is from a family with Republican sympathies, that he lives in the Bogside, that he has approached or been approached by Republicans, or merely that he is broadly sympathetic to the Republican movement. Ciaran is one of a brood of boys in a large family. In one scene we see his tired mother caring for Ciaran and his brothers in the Bogside; with no help from others, she struggles to keep them all out of trouble.

The task of keeping a cadre of young men safe in Derry is formidable when one recognizes that "the security forces' target [for arrest] is primarily Catholic, specifically Catholic men between the ages of 16 and 44" (Jennings et al., 197). According to Jennings and his coauthors, "A staggering 30,444 arrests were made by the army under section 14 [Emergency Provisions Act] between 1975 and the end of 1986. From 1978 to 1986, the police made a further 13,835 arrests under sections 11 and 13, bringing the total for the ten year period to over 44,000. . . . Adding the 6,000 arrests under the Prevention of Terrorism Acts, we arrive at a total of nearly 75,000 arrests in Northern Ireland in the 15 years to the end of 1986" (196–97). Despite the efforts of his mother, Ciaran is taken into custody; because the film is set in the early 1980s, and as Margo Harkin's official synopsis indicates, Ciaran's arrest refers to the "supergrass," paid informer, witness system in Northern Ireland. The year the film was set saw the last stages of the "paid perjurer" system (Harkin 1989).

There are various etymologies of the term "grass," but the term "supergrass" was apparently coined by journalists in a 1970s London case. The supergrass system, however, is used in Germany, Italy, England, and other countries in addition to Northern Ireland. In Ireland supergrass has a long history, but its more contemporary usage has emerged in response to the abolition of internment (1975) and to the limitations placed on the use of confessions in court (1979) (Jennings et al., 74). Supergrass witnesses are products of law enforcement initiatives directed at members of organized or large-scale crime and those who are involved in serious crimes (Jennings et al., 75–76). In Northern Ireland, however, supergrass witnesses create an anomalous system because of the Diplock courts. Although there are no laws concerning supergrass, it is assumed that the "law on accomplice evidence" applies. This law cautions jurors about such witnesses and makes it clear that the testimony of such informers must be carefully evaluated. Because in the North, the Diplock courts disallow trial by jury for certain crimes, presumably the judge(s) must remind himself of the law regarding evidence. Some speculate that judges have not always been so cautious (Jennings et al., 78). Eventually, however, supergrasses were done away with; due to commissioned reports, by 1983 and 1984, supergrass trials were exposed.

After Goretti learns that Ciaran has been taken to jail, she is told not to worry: he will not be imprisoned for long. Goretti's response—"That's what we thought about our Johnny"—indicates that she has known at least one other male, perhaps her brother, who has been imprisoned, and that this experience has made her skeptical about Ciaran's early release. Goretti knows the ritual surrounding incarceration. Although she is understandably eager to meet with him, Goretti cannot obtain a visitor's pass to see Ciaran until his family members have seen him. Each prisoner is allotted a specific number of passes per month or per week; Goretti must wait her turn, and she recognizes and accepts this.

When Goretti finally does visit Ciaran, they meet in a bare room, and a prison guard is present. Ciaran appears nervous as befits both his age and his predicament. When she tells him she is pregnant, Ciaran implies that the pregnancy is Goretti's responsibility, and Goretti leaves the prison hurt and angry. For the remainder of the film, Goretti is alone, and we assume that Ciaran will not be available to help her. Harkin extricates Goretti's story from the narrative of nationalism and situates it instead within the context of the material difficulties that surround her—class, religion, sexuality, and state intervention through the prison. By virtue of its narrative focus on Goretti, the film ceases to participate in cinematic representations of Ireland that examine a male-dominated nationalism. Instead, it foregrounds how nationalism constructs and exacerbates a young Derry woman's already difficult material conditions.

## The Visit

In *Maeve, Mother Ireland,* and *Hush-A-Bye Baby,* the site of the prison sometimes manifests itself only marginally on a cinematic and narrative level. However, when we read within the context of gender and material conditions, we can see that this marginal, almost repressed, site actually initiates the protagonist's movement from an emphasis on nationalism toward a concern for women and their economic and cultural conditions. Yet in *The Visit,* the most recently released of the films analyzed in these two chapters, the prison site is central, and its director, Orla Walsh, acknowledges that the film is informed by the work of Murphy, Crilly, and Harkin. Although we only see the prison in the last few scenes, the site and trope of the jail become a primary focus throughout this short film as the protagonist journeys to visit her husband, a Republican prisoner. In *The Visit* the prison is both the physical site to which the protagonist journeys and the ideological site that prescribes the behavior expected of women who wait outside it. Thus this film goes farther than the others in exploring the role of female family members of those who are incarcerated and in examining how the state and colonial prison demonstrate and exacerbate the confluence of gender and material conditions.

Chronicling the story of what in Northern Ireland is colloquially termed "the wire widow," Walsh's twenty-two-minute film constructs Sheila Molloy's one-day mental and physical journey to visit her husband, Sean, a long-term Republican prisoner in Her Majesty's Prison, the Maze. (Magael MacLaughlin plays the part of Sheila.) Although it is self-consciously indebted to its predecessors, *The Visit* marks an important intervention into women and film because it foregrounds contemporary cultural debates surrounding feminism and Republicanism from *within* the Republican movement (Sheila is married to a Republican and considers herself a part of his community, although she is not a volunteer). It also invokes the prison as a site of woman's emerging consciousness and situates Western feminist film theory within a more complex geopolitical site. For all these reasons, the film explicitly represents the material conditions that impact and construct a woman's life.

Not unlike the previous films discussed, *The Visit* was also difficult to produce. Orla Walsh has said that given the kind of film she wanted to make and the fiscal constraints under which she operated, she decided to create a short film (Sullivan 1997).

Funded with a mere IR£3,500 from the Arts Council (the Republic) and £500 from the Cultural Traditions Groups (Northern Ireland), *The Visit* cost IR£10,000 to produce and is indicative of a history of short filmmaking in the Republic and Northern Ireland. Since there are many people who want to make films and very little money available to them, the genre of the short film has become popular. There are now several colleges and organizations around Dublin that train filmmakers to make short films: Dun Laoghaire College of Art and Design, Dublin City University, Rathmines College, and Film Base. Also, although many movie houses maintain 35 mm projectors, some still utilize 16 mm, and many shorts are made especially for 16 mm projectors.

Orla Walsh received her technical training from and used equipment provided by Film Base and Rathmines College, but *The Visit* is also influenced by one of her earlier ventures: a documentary detailing the Christmas furlough of prisoners from the Maze. After initial screenings of the film, both prisoners and their families lamented the fact that there was little or no discussion of the difficulties encountered by the family members of prisoners, especially wives who were expected to wait patiently and care for their families as their husbands served sentences ranging from ten years to life (Sullivan 1997). With this in mind, Walsh read "The Visit," the short story Lawrence McKeown wrote while he was serving a life sentence in the Maze, and based her film on it.

Through the device of flashbacks, the audience watches the progression of Sheila's emerging consciousness and discovers how she simultaneously supports and critiques the Republican movement but does so through an emphasis on material conditions. In one of the first flashback scenes, we discover that just three weeks after Sheila and Sean are married, he is pulled out of the couple's bed and taken to jail. In this knock-on-the-door scene, as he is being taken away, Sean has only enough time to tell Sheila whom to call for help: "Jesus Christ hold it . . . for fucks sake . . . Sheila, call Sean Kelly." Slowly, Sheila begins to recognize how alone she is, and in the next flashback, she meets her mother. To her mother's admonishments that she "knew there would be trouble," Sheila responds that there are more urgent concerns at hand: "Mammy, for Christ's sake . . . I'm sorry, this isn't the time. He might get twenty years; what will we do?" Sheila's mother does not intend to *do* anything; rather, she hands her daughter IR£40 and says she must "catch the three o'clock train," presumably back to Dublin. Again, we see that material concerns in the North cannot be separated from those in the South. Reluctantly, Sheila's mother becomes involved in the troubles because her daughter does. However, as a Southerner, she will provide money and metaphorically wash her hands of the situation—and of her daughter.

Although Sheila is unprepared for this isolation, she, like Goretti in *Hush-A-Bye Baby*, recognizes what is expected of her. After a short while, Sheila visits Sean's mother, a woman who is obviously experienced in the unspoken rules of incarceration. As the women sit, Sheila is calm, almost catatonic. Behind them are pictures of Mrs. Molloy's sons, and a Republican plaque hangs near a picture of the Sacred Heart of Jesus. Sean's mother inquires about his status: "Is he near Patrick or Joe? Is he sleeping any better now? Last week he said he couldn't sleep for worrying about you. I told him to take care of himself and not to be working himself up about us." Sheila responds, "I know. I told him the same." Patrick and Joe are no doubt Sean's brothers, incarcerated in the same facility and for similar offenses. As the prison narratives examined in chapter 1 indicate, in Northern Ireland it may not be unusual for Republican families to have two or more members incarcerated at the same time.

The cultural role prescribed for women, the role examined in *Mother Ireland* and constructed in part by Patrick Pearse's poem "The Mother," is embodied in Sean's mother: she is the mother who will offer her sons for the good of a United Ireland; Mrs. Molloy has given three of her sons to "the cause." The first few lines of Pearse's poem suggest how mothers should behave: "I do not grudge them: Lord, I do not grudge / My two strong sons that I have seen go out . . . And yet I have my joy: / My sons were faithful, and they fought." She has internalized the messages of maternal self-sacrifice, which takes on a particular guise in the context of the struggle for a United Ireland: "I told him to take care of himself and not to be working himself up about us." With this statement, Sean's mother suggests not only that she is doing her part but also that she expects Sheila to do the same. Sheila does not need to be reminded, however, and we watch the scene and acknowledge just how well this "wire widow" does know what is expected of her.

Finally, Sean's mother asks what she has been wondering: "Look. He won't tell me. Is he going on the blanket?" Calmly Sheila notes that "of course; you knew he'd want to." Sheila knows that Sean's mother is already aware that her son will engage in this protest, because, as a Republican prisoner, this is what is expected of him. Later, when Sheila refuses the behavior expected of a "wire widow," she will refer back to this protest. For now, though, these initial scenes serve both to indicate how Sheila will critique Republicanism and/or nationalism, and to suggest that she is firmly established within this movement: she knows what is expected of her.

In *The Visit* Walsh makes explicit the characters' connection to Republicanism. Sean is willing to protest prison conditions because he is a Republican. Sheila makes use of Republican-provided transportation: when she visits Sean, she rides in the van provided by Sinn Fein. Family members of those wrongly imprisoned for Republican activity or those who do not claim a Republican status will not ride in the van. The film thus focuses our attention on material conditions—transportation, state intervention, sexuality, the usefulness of the Irish language, and the women's movement— from *within* Republicanism.

The film's construction of the debate between feminism and Republicanism is significant not only because the terms of this debate are critiqued from within the movement but also because women's relation to Republicanism may serve to complicate the terms of feminist movements and feminist theory in Northern Ireland and elsewhere. Although the issues of women and the Republican movement and women and nationalism have been discussed at some length by scholars, Republicans, and feminists, two recent pamphlets highlight the lines along which such discussions are drawn and suggest the stakes involved for the women's movement and feminist theory.

In "From Cathleen to Anorexia: The Breakdown of Irelands," Edna Longley focuses on the ideological breakdown of nationalism, a disintegration which she likens to the ideological breakdown of an Irish feminism that has as its center the image of Cathleen Ni Houlihan or Dark Rosaleen. Longley discusses the failures of nationalism and then moves to an explicit critique of Republicanism and women in the Republican movement. She is critiquing a version of anti-imperialist discourse and notes that in the early twentieth century, during the Irish revolution, "nationalist women discovered . . . that their oppression as women did not end with the Dawning of the Day" (181). Furthermore, she contends that "as a general rule: the more Republican, the less Feminist" (181). Longley extends this argument into the present day and states that Sinn Fein women "cling, like their elder sisters, to the prospective goodwill of the republican men, and to the fallacy that: 'there can't be women's liberation until there's national liberation'"(182). Finally, she insists that "it remains true that the vast majority of Republican women come from traditionally Republican families—recruited by and for a patriarchal unit" (182). Although she productively suggests that in the past Republican women have found themselves in inadequate positions after conflict resolution, Longley fails to analyze whether or not this results from gender and class inconsistencies. She "blames" Republican men and simultaneously fails to acknowledge the specific ways women are oppressed.

In "Sex and Nation: Women in Irish Culture and Politics," Gerardine Meaney urges an examination not only of the conditions under which women become Republicans but also of the lessons such women can teach all feminists. According to Meaney, her purpose is to "challenge the assumptions made by and about the women's movement in Ireland" (188); to accomplish this, she must discuss Republicanism, nationalism, Unionism, and also Longley's article. Meaney contends that for many women in Northern Ireland, both feminism and a version of nationalism are positive forces for change. She states that "Edna Longley's denial that it is impossible to be both feminist and republican is not only an historical absurdity, it runs the risk of making Irish feminism no more than a middle class movement directed towards equal par-tic-ipation [*sic*] by privileged women in the status quo" (195). Al-though Meaney encourages an interrogation of nationalism and Republicanism, she also advocates that feminists listen carefully before they so quickly denigrate Republican women: "Instead of lecturing Republican women on their political and moral failings as women we might pause to listen. Perhaps they could teach us to address those women for whom the myth of Mother Ireland is still a powerful enchantment" (196). Meaney's article fruitfully ex-plores the connections between feminism and Republicanism, and her examination of this relation suggests a path forward for femi-nists; to learn from Republican women, while critiquing the ideol-ogy to which they subscribe, will ensure more equitable and less elitist feminist movements.

Orla Walsh's film participates in the debate outlined by Longley and Meaney, because this film constructs a woman who is not sim-ply "created by and for a patriarchal unit"; rather, Sheila Molloy is a woman who chooses to remain in the Republican movement but also to critique this movement. Sheila's two most pronounced cri-tiques of Republicanism and a version of nationalism center on the concepts of motherhood and paid employment. At the beginning of her journey to visit her husband, Sheila walks past a mural on the Falls Road: on the wall is painted a woman; next to her is the Sinn Fein slogan (originally articulated by Bobby Sands, the hun-ger striker who died in Long Kesh, the Maze Prison), "Everyone, Republican or Otherwise Has Her/His Role to Play." As Sheila has demonstrated from the time her husband was arrested until the present, she is well aware of the "role" she is expected to play; yet throughout the remainder of the film, we watch as she questions the confines of this role.

Sheila most obviously questions and then critiques her role as the "wire widow" when, after her husband has been incarcerated for seven years, she has an affair and becomes pregnant. When she tells her lover of her condition, he asks her to run away to Dublin with him. Sheila is vehement in her refusal and states that "this whole thing [the affair, the pregnancy] was never about you or him [Sean]. It was about me. Everything has always been decided for me. Now I'm going to have a life for myself. A new life with this child." When her lover reminds Sheila that her community/the Republican community will shun her, she states that now she will see whether or not her husband and others will stand by the women who do so much for them. She notes that "if this is a problem for people they'll have to deal with it. The same with Sean. I stood by him through it all—the blanket, the dirt and the deaths. Now I'll see if he's got the strength to stand by me." The fact that Sheila stood by Sean during the aforementioned strikes is significant not only because she did what was expected of her but also because there was some controversy concerning family members during the hunger strikes.

As Barbara Harlow explains, although there was popular support for the strikers, family members were often pressured by state authority to urge prisoners to cease the strikes. Harlow provocatively suggests that this pressure indicated the role family members, especially women, were asked to play: "The issue of the family, particularly as 'family' is construed through the role conventionally played by wives and mothers in defining and maintaining traditional familial coherence and ideological integrity, is central to the resistance narrative of the hunger strike" (92). Not unlike Goretti, whose Irish dictionary defines a mother only as that which carries a family, Irish women were seen by the church and state as solely the nurturers of their families and were asked to use this role for the state's purpose.

Whereas the state used women's constructed role as nurturers to encourage them to pressure their sons, husbands, brothers, and lovers to cease the hunger strikes, the Republican movement used this role to encourage women to support their male relatives at all costs. Sheila supported Sean through the hunger strikes, thus reifying the role of the family that such support constructs. When Sheila becomes pregnant and insists that she will determine whether or not Sean and the Republican community will support her, not only is she asserting herself as a woman, but she is also questioning the traditional concept of family that her support of the hunger strikes initially reinforced. The family Sheila is proposing is one conceived with a man who is not her husband, and conceived while her husband is imprisoned. Sheila is reconstructing a version of family and thereby altering the traditional familial structure of Republicanism.

Sheila's desire to ascertain whether or not her husband and their community will support her suggests that if they will, she will make the decision to remain, as a pregnant women, in the community; that decision signals a further debate: the debate from within the movement concerning reproductive rights. Some feminists in Northern Ireland insist that although because of political tensions and allegiances women in the region often have difficulty reaching a consensus on an issue, they have unified in an effort to work toward reproductive rights. According to Eileen Evason, the Northern Ireland women's rights movement sometimes galvanized around the issue of reproductive freedom: "For much of the 1970s abortion was an unmentionable subject in Northern Ireland. . . . The Northern Ireland Abortion campaign organised the first conference to deal with the subject in 1980. In the same year the group secured substantial media coverage when 600 coat-hangers were sent to the House of Commons [London]. Each had a British Airways ticket attached and a message to MPs which read 'these are the two ways in which Northern Ireland women get abortions'" (27). Evason's statement reminds us that although abortion legislation was extended to the United Kingdom in 1972, because of international political and religious pressures, it has not yet been guaranteed in Northern Ireland. Evason's words also indicate that although there have always been political pressures that have rendered it difficult for women in Northern Ireland to agree on explicitly feminist agendas, some women have united to discuss the issue of reproductive rights. Yet Sheila Molloy might not have been one of the women of which Evason speaks. Walsh's film suggests that feminists must learn to listen to and learn from Republican women such as Sheila whose feminist agenda may be different.

Sheila's choice calls for an examination of the Republican movement's policy on abortion, a policy which reminds us that perhaps not all women in Northern Ireland would be able to unite over the issue of reproductive rights. According to "Women in Ireland" (1992), the *Sinn Fein Women's Policy Document,* Sinn Fein urges a woman's right to choose, but this document also reveals the organization's ideological roots in both Catholicism and an electoral party system: "Sinn Fein is opposed to the attitudes and forces in society that compel women to have abortions, and which criminalises those who do. We accept the need for abortion where a woman's life is at risk or grave danger (e.g. all forms of cancer) and in cases of rape or child sexual abuse" ("Women in Ireland" 1992). The first line does much to suggest the culpability of the state and social forces in the choices a woman is allowed to make; the latter portion, however, reinforces a rigid allocation of choice—one based not upon a woman's right to her body, but rather upon the redress she is entitled to after some external force (that is, illness or violence) has harmed this corporeality. Yet this particular policy document reveals more than Catholic ideology; it also denotes a Republican fear of its electorate.

In an interview with Laura Lyons, Mairead Keane, then national head of Sinn Fein Women's Department, discusses the policy document, Sinn Fein, and reproductive rights. Keane notes that the Women's Department emerged as nationalist women became increasingly aware of their feminist consciousness, and she insists that women became cognizant of their oppression as women as a result of the "actual political activity on the ground" (quoted in Lyons, 272). In other words, women became more aware of gender oppression through their consciousness of national oppression. For Keane, Republican women are Republicans first, women second. Keane also reads the right-to-choose question as that which will suggest women's diverse views on political activity: many women will want access to abortion, while others will not see this as a major issue for national liberation. Those in the latter category will think that the most important thing is for Northern Ireland to be liberated from British rule; those in the former will see women's rights as tied to national rights. Keane explains that when the "right to choose" motion was "put forward in 1986 or 1987 by Sinn Fein in Derry, . . . it was passed, but it also led to problems for us politically, because we are not a major party" (quoted in Lyons, 265). According to Keane, because Sinn Fein is not a major party, it could not advance such a motion. She suggests that the issue of reproductive choice posed problems for Sinn Fein, and that, therefore, the party should have mobilized under the "right to information" position (that is, information on where to obtain an abortion). Her discussion of the debate indicates both the diverse opinions regarding reproductive rights in Sinn Fein and the Republican movement, and the party politics involved in these opinions.

Such debates would not have been lost on the character of Sheila Molloy. Her decision to question but also to remain within the Republican movement, along with her desire to bring a pregnancy to term while recognizing that she may be caring for this child alone in a difficult community, indicates that women within the Republican movement may not be merely handmaidens of a patriarchal unit, as some would have it. Rather, such women may espouse a political allegiance unintelligible within the hegemonic discourse of Western feminism. Furthermore, in the larger (state-controlled) political arena, the issue of reproductive rights is inextricably bound with what are more broadly defined as political issues of electoral party considerations and economic and religious configurations. Similarly, in Sinn Fein and in Republican ideology, the issue of reproductive rights is tied to other political concerns such as whether or not Sinn Fein has the numbers to advance such a platform. Feminists who seek to imagine what newly configured Northern Ireland will emerge after conflict resolution might acknowledge this. Sheila's decision to bring her pregnancy to term is significant, because this decision is a critique of nationalism and/or Republican ideology.

Yet Sheila also critiques the Republican movement in another manner: she questions the usefulness of the Irish language for nationalism. In her critique, Sheila will use the Irish language for the *material*—as opposed to *nationalist*—benefits it will allow. Sheila's husband, Sean, speaks of learning Irish in prison ("we have our Open University exam next week"); for him the language provides an opportunity for Republican solidarity and resistance. Yet for Sheila, a volunteer at a local primary school, the language carries a more material purpose. During one of her visits, Sheila tells her husband that she wants to go to Donegal in the summer because "they say if I can improve my Irish they'll take me on full time." Here Sheila explicitly extricates the Irish language from the rhetoric of nationalism and places it in the realm of material conditions. The Irish language offers her an opportunity to make money and support herself! Even if the Irish language does provide Sean a sense of solidarity, his mastery of it will not pay Sheila's rent.

While Sheila and Sean have diverse views on the uses of the Irish language, the abovementioned scene does indicate that Republican prisoners avail themselves of Open University/adult education courses. Although some in Ireland insist that Republican men fail to recognize feminist principles, *The Visit* widens the debate to suggest that at least some Republican men have begun to acknowledge feminist concerns. If they have, this could complicate arguments that insist Republicanism does not/will not/cannot attend to issues of gender.

In her interview with Mairead Keane, Laura Lyons inquires about Republican men and prison education. Mairead Keane maintains that Sinn Fein Women's Department helps men, particularly those in jail, understand "how feminism forwards the equality of men and women . . . and how that actually gets translated in people's real lives" (quoted in Lyons, 279). She insists that prisoners want to learn about feminism because "they are politically minded people in a revolution that involves feminism as part of that movement" (quoted in Lyons, 278).

Lawrence McKeown's "The Visit" originally appeared in the summer 1990 issue of *The Captive Voice/An Glor Gafa*. In one of the first issues of this Republican magazine, the editorial board defines its scope: "For some . . . struggle is seen only in terms of direct militant action which attacks the most overt manifestations of oppression, such as the armies of the state. . . . one of the aims of *An Glor Gafa* is to challenge this exclusive view of struggle, and its pages have given a brief insight into the extent and type of struggle facing Irish people daily; struggles against the oppression of women, against cultural oppression, against the destruction of the environment." Written by and primarily for Republican prisoners, *The Captive Voice/An Glor Gafa* describes the Republican struggle as one defined less exclusively by a military impetus and more fully by the cultural and economic conditions under which people live. In the summer 1990 issue of the magazine, the editors delimit this focus even further:

This issue of *An Glor Gafa/The Captive Voice* highlights the oppression of women—and in particular women POWs [most specifically Republican female prisoners]. At a time when a young woman was so brutally gang-raped in the heart of a nationalist area and when there has been a marked increase in the incidents of sexual assault on women, it is particularly relevant that we address ourselves to the issue of women's oppression. While many facets of this can be generalized under the term "inequality of opportunity" or explained away by referring to how we were all brought up to accept the "natural" position of women (and men) within society, men must question their present attitudes, views and behaviour towards women. (1)

In *Barred: Women, Writing, and Political Detention*, Barbara Harlow contends that formal and informal prison education is necessarily subversive as it undermines the very walls and premises that contain it (23). The magazine mentioned above is one way for Republicans to educate one another. While her study does not specifically examine whether or not what men learn in prison remains with them after they are released, Harlow does suggest that prison education alters the direction of the patriarchal family along with the patriarchal construction of resistance organizations, and also reverses state authority. Prison education's most productive possibility includes altering the direction of resistance organizations and state institutions: "The experience of prison—from state apparatus to prison counterculture, and its impact on the larger society—proposes new priorities and agendas for political organizing and cultural mobilization, with critical implications for altering the curricula of other public institutions as well" (Harlow, 22). As Harlow's work and the pages of *The Captive Voice/ An Glor Gafa* reveal, the assumption that Republican women are merely passive victims of a Republican patriarchy must be reevaluated in light of an educational process that began in part as a result of female agitation within Sinn Fein and the Republican movement.

If feminists intend to examine the positions in which all women will be placed after conflict resolution, they should be more sensitive to women within political movements often deemed merely patriarchal. These movements may very well be oppressive to women, but feminists must also acknowledge the possibilities some women believe they do afford. In other words, although many feminists conjecture that nationalism and Republicanism oppress women, and although the texts examined in this book often demonstrate this as well, not all women recognize these ideologies as oppressive. Feminists need to learn why.

While Sean's statement that he participates in Open University courses is significant for its emphasis on the possibilities of prison education for women and men, this statement also signals another problematic with which Republican and/or nationalist women in Northern Ireland must contend. Sean mentions his adult education classes when he and Sheila are discussing Sheila's work plans. Just after Sheila notes that she wants to travel to Donegal to improve her Irish, Sean is immediately suspicious: "Who would you go with? I hope not with that one Debbie; I hear she is a real slag." Sheila correctly responds that Debbie is just a young girl having a bit of fun. "That's still allowed isn't it?" asks Sheila. Yet Sean's question indicates the level of surveillance under which women are placed. Sean hears that Debbie is a "slag." He learns this information because there is an elaborate network of surveillance under which women's actions are watched and reported (not always maliciously but certainly intrusively) to prisoners. Male prisoners have explained that spreading and listening to gossip helps pass the time and makes them feel connected to the outside world (Campbell et al.); however, for women this gossip is clearly intrusive. The extent to which "wire widows" are watched is suggested in two other scenes.

In the first, Sheila and three of her female friends relax at a Republican club; while couples dance around them, the women laugh and talk. At one point Sheila instructs one of the women about making prison parcels and offers to change her day to see Sean if the woman needs help with her initial visit to the prison. Soon the women notice that they are being eyed by three men at the bar and that one of them seems anxious: "Look at the state of your man!" one of them jokes. The camera pans the men and focuses on two drinkers who are encouraging a third to approach the women. As the third man makes a move to do so, one of the other two tells him that "they're all prisoners' wives." The third quickly turns back in fear, because he knows that one of the unspoken rules is that men must not approach the wives of prisoners; if they do, this will certainly get back to the husbands. (The man Sheila eventually has an affair with is from Dublin and does not understand these rules; for example, when Sheila initially refuses to go out for a pint with him, he is confused and annoyed, and says, "You're not the one in prison.")

Although this pub scene speaks to the surveillance under which women are placed, the scene that most obviously details the extent to which prisoners' wives and all women are watched by their community occurs when Sheila is in the prison visitors' waiting room. She overhears two women discuss the misfortune of a third: "It's a pity about Theresa Lynch. [She had] beautiful hair too. They said it was for shoplifting, but I heard it was for playing around." Although many have suggested that Republicans no longer tar and feather girls who become (or are suspecting of becoming) involved with British soldiers and RUC officers, this scene at least *constructs* the fear of reprisal (either physical or emotional) with which women must contend. Additionally, the woman's statement that "they said it was for shoplifting" refers to the fact that the IRA sometimes takes it upon itself to punish community members who commit crimes.

In yet another scene, women question Sheila's deviation from her visitation schedule: "I thought you go to see Sean on Wednesday?" Because women are so often under surveillance, they begin to watch one another.

Women from within the Republican community not only are continually watched by their community members but also are under constant surveillance by the state on the streets and inside the prison grounds. Indeed, one of the most striking aspects of the film is the extent to which Sheila Molloy is watched by the state's gaze(s). It is the context of this gaze that compels a reconsideration of feminist film theory. While in *Maeve* the pub scene focuses on the fact that the gaze actually is owned by Republican men and, by association, state forces, in *Anne Devlin* and *Hush-A-Bye Baby* we also see how women are watched by men. Yet in *The Visit* the prison and its visible cameras (at times the director's camera focuses on the prison cameras) are central to the action. Additionally, because we see Sheila continually followed by the "eyes" of both the security cameras and British soldiers in Belfast, the film compels a return to an analysis of the gaze, specifically as this gaze *is* owned by the state and by the Republican movement.

The gazes upon Sheila are foreshadowed at the beginning of the film. As she prepares for her journey, Sheila looks at herself in her flat mirror and steadies herself for the day ahead. In contemporary British and American feminist film theory, a woman's gaze into the mirror is significant, for it signals her construction by men or the male look. In her oft-discussed "Visual Pleasure and Narrative Cinema," Laura Mulvey reads psychoanalysis to determine how the unconscious of a patriarchal society has structured cinematic form: "In a world ordered by sexual imbalance, pleasure in looking has been split between active/male and passive/female. The determining male gaze projects its phantasy on to the female figure which is styled accordingly" (1988, 62). For Mulvey, the gaze is incontrovertibly male because the male projects his fantasy of femininity onto women.

But where, Mulvey wants to know, did feminist British film theory begin? Where it began has much to do with how the gaze is identified. In "British Feminist Film Theory's Female Spectators: Presence and Absence," Laura Mulvey traces a genealogy of British feminist film theory. She argues that it was inspired by the women's liberation workshops and what she terms the "high theory" strand of British feminist theory, influenced by the *New Left Review*'s break with "the specific Englishness of British left culture and politics" (1989, 69). According to Mulvey, Britain "looked to France for theory and Hollywood cinema for critical raw material" (1989, 69). British feminist film theory was also influenced by the introduction of Hollywood cinema into Britain; the women's movement's concern with (negative) images of women; and the "return" of avant-garde cinema to Britain's culture. Importantly, Mulvey states that by the mid-1970s, the British Film Institute Production Board began to support the cinema that emerged as a consequence of this climate. This is very significant if we remember that Northern Ireland was not a recognized region of the British Film Institute, though Britain did fund Irish film. While British feminist film theory was being defined within an imperial space, Northern Ireland was mostly absent from the discussion. Throughout the 1970s at least, there had been some discussion about film from the Republic. However, to my knowledge, there was never an explicitly Irish feminist agenda discussed in the genealogy provided by Mulvey. Given this rupture, dominant theories of the gaze will not necessarily be intelligible within Northern Ireland or the Republic. The male gaze as it was defined by British film theory was a gaze defined without benefit of the particulars of Northern Ireland; thus a different version of feminist cinematic readings of the gaze could both inform and be informed by film made about or in the North.

In this mirror scene, Sheila's image is reflected in the mirror, but her eyes are *always elsewhere*, signaling that she must always be conscious of the gaze of others (lurking) around her. In this scene, Sheila does not look straight back into the mirror: she can never merely look at herself; she must always watch what is around her. She has to do both at the same time because she is always being watched—by her community and by the state. Feminist film theory, which reads this surveillance as always male, is brought to a halt. Feminists are still assuming an analysis based on the philosophically and psychoanalytically constructed subject. Sheila Molloy's gaze into the mirror complicates these analyses by suggesting that for women in (post)colonial locations, the look is always already elsewhere. Sheila's look is never a gaze foisted upon herself by an unspecified "other" or by the male unconscious; rather, it is a gaze that is materially present around her in the looks of her community and the state. There may not, for example, be a military presence in her bedroom, but moments before Sheila looks into this mirror, she listens to a radio broadcast of RUC activity. Moreover, it was not an unowned gaze that was once in her bedroom taking her husband to prison. It was a particular military gaze and body. Sheila's glance not only at but also around and outside of the mirror anticipates the surveillance cameras she will encounter when she walks out of her flat; later, she will be watched by the prison center's camera as well as cameras in Belfast. So rather than suggesting a collective male gaze, as British and American feminist film theory would have it, these gazes are owned by specific men, men who are engaged in paramilitary organizations and state forces, and by Sheila's community.

Feminist film theory can learn much by recognizing the state's gaze upon Sheila. Early in her journey, when Sheila is waiting to be picked up by the (Republican-provided) van, two soldiers leer at her. Dressed in camouflage and sporting automatic machine guns, these young soldiers watch Sheila walk toward her destination and continue to leer once she has arrived. When she counters their looks with her own, the camera moves to the security camera above her to remind audiences that she cannot merely reverse the gaze of the "other"; another state gaze will watch her from above. *The Visit* acknowledges this and seeks not merely to reverse a gaze but rather to ascertain the specific material cause of it: who is looking and what is the effect of the look?

Throughout Belfast, security cameras are perched atop buildings, in doorways, over street signs, and next to houses, indicating that the state gaze is always upon women in Northern Ireland; the gaze of the state is upon Sheila when she enters the prison grounds as well. When Walsh's camera first pans this site, the audience sees the large security tower behind the prison's barbed wire fence. And throughout the film, we watch as Land Rovers and army vehicles equipped with telephoto lenses crawl through the streets of downtown Belfast. Sheila's look in her mirror, then, is both a look at herself and always also at that which is looking at her.

For Walsh, the audience is also looking. When we identify our eyes with the eye of Walsh's camera, the watchful community, and the state gaze, we are acknowledging that we need to "look" at

Walsh's protagonist and how she critiques Republicanism but nevertheless will (if allowed) remain a part of this movement.

As we have seen, feminist film in Northern Ireland questions the nationalist narrative. Also, through their focus on the site of the prison, women in the North force a reconsideration of their material needs. In *Maeve, Anne Devlin, Mother Ireland, Hush-A-Bye Baby,* and *The Visit* women are constructed as those figures who critique Republican and/or nationalist ideology; they are also assumed to be a force that may suggest the path forward for women after conflict resolution. Ultimately, however, each of these films does analyze one or more characters, even though these characters may represent the plight of women more generally. Charabanc Theatre Company illustrates the material needs of women now and in the future. Yet rather than analyzing specific characters, it speaks about collective material conditions in Northern Ireland.

# "Politics, That's the Nub of It": Charabanc Theatre Company and the (Collective) Economy of Production

Carter, the American director of a Northern Irish reconciliation center, encourages women to look closely at the beauty which surrounds them: "nature . . . the beauty of nature . . . and it's ours to enjoy. Through nature we can find ourselves. It is something that is in all of us and belongs to all of us." Veronica, a Northern Irish woman visiting the center, replies, "You're dead lucky though, Carter. When I look out my window, I see a dirty great big wall with 'Fuck the UVF' written on it." (Charabanc Theatre Company, *Now You're Talkin'*)

The shifting distinctions between representation within the state and political economy, on the one hand, and within the theory of the Subject on the other, must not be obliterated. . . . My view is that radical practice should attend to this double version of representations rather than reintroduce the individual subject.

(Gayatri Spivak, "Can the Subaltern Speak?")

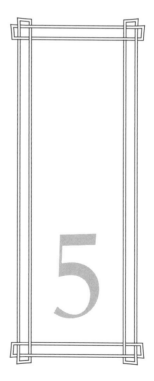

ALTHOUGH CHARABANC THEATRE COMPANY has received international acclaim, most of its plays remain unpublished. Therefore, many scholars who analyze Charabanc's work have been content to introduce the company or question why so little drama by women has been published. In his interesting article on theater by women in the Republic and Northern Ireland, Steve Wilmer both introduces Charabanc and notes the company's good fortune in being one of the few theater groups to have actually received funding in the North (358). In "Charabanc Theatre Company: Placing Women Center-Stage in Northern Ireland," Maria DiCenzo reminds readers not only that Charabanc's funding was always provisional but also that often women's plays do not get published (176–77). She also correctly takes to task D. E. S. Maxwell's survey of mostly male Northern Irish playwrights and his characterization of drama by women as "domestic plays."

Perhaps taking for granted that their audience is familiar with Charabanc, in *Theatre Ireland* Caroline Williams and Kathleen Quinn analyze the company and question the lack of published female playwrights on the island. Yet Quinn also acknowledges the "upsurge" in women who have written plays in the 1980s and 1990s and understands this increase in the context of the fairly recent emergence of theater groups founded and cofounded by women: Druid, Focus, Big Telly, Charabanc, and Glasshouse, just to name a few (10). Yet in the end, Victoria White's provocative *Theatre Ireland* article entitled "Cathleen Ni Houlihan Is Not a Playwright" dares to make the connection between the dearth of published plays by women and the context of drama in the Republic of Ireland. White states, "Politics. That's the nub of it. We have continued as Pearse began. The only woman revered is the Mother Ireland who informs the Proclamation of the Republic. The Constitution says 'See Family, Sex' when you look up 'woman' in the index, and promises to safeguard her place within the home. Our politics have, until recently, mirrored this ideology, consisting of clashes between two sides of an old war as to the particular cast Mother Ireland is to have, rather than [discuss] real economic issues. Our theatre . . . has mirrored this ideology as well" (29).

White is referring to article 41.2 of the 1937 Constitution, Republic of Ireland.

Article 41.2 applauds women's essential role as homemakers, thereby making it less likely that they will be seen as employees or artists, for example. White is also referring to the ideology of Mother Ireland articulated by Patrick Pearse and others. In a poem he wrote just before he was executed for his part in the Easter Rising of 1916, Pearse wrote about his mother and, by association, all of Ireland's mothers, wives, sisters, and lovers. As has already been stated, Pearse wrote about the woman who was willing to give her son selflessly for the good of Ireland. Coupled with the 1937 constitution, this ideology of maternal sacrifice has kept us from recognizing "real" women and their needs. White acknowledges that rather than question or interrogate the images of women outlined by Pearse and encoded in the constitution, Irish theater has merely reinforced it. White argues that we must examine the way women are represented in theater and explore the material (economic) conditions that beset them. Only then, she implies, will we be prepared to understand women in Ireland, their representation in Irish theater and Irish drama itself.

Charabanc Theatre Company explores the material conditions that impact women's lives. The company focuses on economic and cultural conditions in Northern Ireland by shifting the focus from the individual to the community. In the community, issues such as internment and illegal activity are important concerns. Yet the company also examines other material conditions such as divorce, domestic abuse, pregnancy, and the conflict in Northern Ireland. Ultimately, the conflict in the North becomes just one more, albeit one large, burden with which women must contend. Again, nationalism does not define women; rather, they are concerned about their material needs, needs which are informed and in some cases exacerbated by nationalism but are not reducible to this ideology.

Recognizing that poststructuralist critics who analyze power-knowledge relations leave intact what she terms the "West as Subject" and the "Western Subject," and given that such critics also neglect the urgencies of global capitalism, Gayatri Spivak proposes an alternative method of theorizing. She argues that we can gain little by reifying the subject and must move instead toward an analysis of how the subject is represented and constructed within the state and political economy, where the state is a marker of geopolitics and the political economy refers to global capitalism. The reason for her distinction is clear: when we look at representation—rather than only at the individual subject—we will no longer need to locate heroes and individual agents of power, all participants in colonial expansion and the imperial project. Instead, we will be able to recognize the forces that construct the individual and create oppression. Yet in order to move from an analysis of the subject to an understanding of the political economy, we must recognize, as Spivak puts it, that "the relationship between global capitalism (exploitation in economics) and nation-state alliances (domination in geo-politics) is so macrological that it cannot account for the micrological texture of power. To move toward such an accounting one must move toward theories of ideology—of subject formations that micrologically and often erratically operate the interests that congeal the macrologies" (1988b, 279).

Spivak is not merely calling for a discursive analysis of the subject but rather for a trenchant examination of the ideological formulation of the subject as she is constructed through local and global capital. She wants us to examine the economic exploitation of women, because for Spivak, such exploitation is caused by national and international capital. When it speaks less of individual subjects and more of collective concerns, Charabanc forces us to consider women and material conditions.

For Charabanc, women in Northern Ireland are constructed by inadequate property laws, lack of reproductive choice, inequality in the workplace, and domestic abuse. They are constructed within the political economy through their relationship to labor, police, and paramilitary forces. Finally, they are constructed by institutions controlled by colonial and state forces, institutions such as the prison system. Charabanc's *Lay Up Your Ends* (1983) dramatizes the Belfast linen workers' strike in the early part of this century and establishes the company's emphasis upon women and material conditions such as (un)employment. *Now You're Talkin'* (1985) mocks state and (inter)national forces that struggle to find a solution to the conflict in Northern Ireland but which do so by neglecting the concerns of women. Finally, *Somewhere over the Balcony* (1987) takes to task institutions such as marriage, British and Northern Irish surveillance techniques, and internment, all forces which impact women's daily lives.

## Collective Beginnings

From its inception, Charabanc, which translates as an "open tour bus," has conceived of itself as a collective: a group of five unemployed female actors who want to write in and about Northern Ireland for an international stage. For some time the company's primary writer, Marie Jones, has said that Charabanc began as a result of the dearth of good female roles available in the North. Importantly, Jones links the group's collective female composition to economic circumstances: "At that time [1983, when the group was founded] anybody who was in Belfast was going to be working or they'd go off to London or somewhere else. . . . we had no money. All we had was an idea and love, commitment, and excitement. It was very hard to get men to go along with that" (quoted in Martin, 90).

According to recent statistics, 11.8 percent of Northern Ireland's male workforce is unemployed, but the rate of unemployment in particular communities is much more dramatic, with Catholic communities disproportionately affected: Strabane in County Tyrone has 23.2 percent unemployment; Newry, 21.9 percent; Derry, 21.8 percent; and Cookston, 18.5 percent (*Irish Times* 1995). Given the high rate of unemployment in the North, Charabanc could obviously have found some male actors.

Yet some men were employed in at least part-time or temporary or "one-off" schemes while women were unemployed; also, Charabanc wanted to provide work for females, particularly Irish females. According to Charlotte Headrick in "'Moving a Mountain with a Spoon': The Circle Is Unbroken, Personal Narratives into Political Drama: Charabanc's *Lay Up Your Ends*," the women were tired of seeing television, film, and theater roles in the Republic and Northern Ireland given to English actresses, and wanted to create roles for themselves. In fact, this first play speaks both to the position of women in 1911 during Belfast's York Street Mills Strike and to the predicament of Charabanc women in 1983: both sets of females were either underemployed or unemployed.

Built on the foundation of economic disadvantage, Charabanc recognized the material concerns of others in Northern Ireland and quickly acknowledged its desire to perform theater for and about one group: the working class. The group's emphasis on the working class is obvious in the dialect of *Lay Up Your Ends*. The play is based on an older, working-class dialect, one with which even the women of Charabanc were initially unfamiliar (7). In one of its earliest programs, Charabanc indicates its wish to produce plays of and for the Protestant and Catholic working-class communities in which its members live. In this program, Charabanc states its goals: to devise plays from and for the communities in which its members live; to commission new Irish writing; and to introduce and reinterpret existing texts (*Charabanc Theatre Company*). Jones emphasizes the group's class specificity when she notes that although the company has been called feminist, Charabanc does not define itself as such because that would be to "alienate the community" (quoted in Martin, 97): "We've been fighting for three and one half years to say we're a working-class theatre company" (quoted in Martin, 97). Interestingly, it is more acceptable for this theater group to call itself working-class than feminist, even though it addresses both class and gender concerns. In a region where it has been publicly deemed more acceptable to discuss the "broad" political problems of class and national affiliation, gender has had to take a backseat. Indeed, according to feminists, women have been encouraged to subsume their concerns as women to what has been seen as the more important national problem: the war or conflict. As noted in chapter 4, the women's movement was divided over this issue. No doubt the theater group feels it will be more acceptable for it to claim a class as opposed to a gendered identity in the North; the company may also recognize class issues as being more prominent than gender concerns. Yet, however the group defines itself, Charabanc's plays exhibit a commitment to class as well as gender concerns.

Collective concerns have translated into collaborative writing. As a group, Charabanc researches material and interviews Belfast citizens for information for its plays. For *Lay Up Your Ends,* the women of Charabanc worked from a newspaper clipping of a wildcat strike in the York Street Mills in Belfast. They then interviewed women in their community who had worked in the mills, and conducted research about the period. Later, they asked Martin Lynch to help them write the play. According to Carol Martin in "Charabanc Theatre Company," this collaborative writing means that "although conceived and written by Charabanc, the plays deny individual authorship by being taken directly from taped interviews with Catholic and Protestant women and men from Northern Irish society" (89). Collaborative writing reinforces the company's focus on collective identity; it is not writing about one woman and her "take" on Northern Ireland, but rather on many women and their collective material conditions.

The group's collective composition, and self-conscious evocation of the material—economic, cultural—conditions under which it operates, consistently contest bourgeois theater's emphasis on individual growth and catharsis. One example of Charabanc's refusal of bourgeois theater is evidenced by the fact that when its members are in Northern Ireland, the group stages productions in community centers and small theaters where there is one flat ticket price and, theoretically, nonhierarchical seating. Although the group's rejection of bourgeois drama in favor of ostensibly more egalitarian theater is indebted to political theater in the vein of Bertold Brecht and others, Charabanc is different because it focuses explicitly on women's concerns.

*Lay Up Your Ends* (1983), written by Martin Lynch and the company and directed by Pam Brighton, was Charabanc's first production. It was first staged in the Belfast Civic Arts Theatre on May 15, 1983. The play opens with five female linen workers singing a mill song, a song they have adapted to include the specific cast of characters who comprise their workplace:

> . . . who'd be a Belfast spinner,
> feet in the water all day,
> Tie up your bands, hawk up your
> yarn, pick out the laps,
> Wet Belfast Mill.
>
> Look out for the spinning master,
> Houl your carry on,
> Whisht to your songs and chatter,
> When Jim Doran's around,
> Mind your frame, look to your
> yarn, lay up your ends,
> Grey Belfast Mill. (I.i)

The phrase "lay up your ends" is a mill term that means to tie up broken threads. The York Street Mill Strike, encouraged by the Marxist reformer James Connolly, was not successful in terms of its original goal: preventing shorter hours and, therefore, less pay. The strikers also protested that if there were to be shorter hours, they should have Saturdays off. Finally, the workers wanted unfair fines and regulations taken away. Nevertheless, after the strike, on September 5, 1911, the first women's branch of the Irish Transport and General Workers' Union was founded. For my purposes, however, what is significant about this play is that it underscores how women are created by the mill economy and unemployment concerns in the North and how women fight back as a group intent on alleviating inadequate material conditions.

The play focuses on one group of women strikers, friends of different religious backgrounds whose initial individual dialogues are meant to suggest how the Irish state and international politics inform their class status. The scenes that focus on individual characters are not represented in conventional realist terms (sometimes, for example, the women are presented as mirages or their words are self-consciously uttered); thus we are encouraged not to read the characters as individual women so much as representations of how women have been constructed by economic and political forces in Northern Ireland.

Florrie, the first character we see, is originally from the country and moves to Belfast after her mother dies. As a young woman, she undertakes the emotional and financial responsibility of raising her younger siblings. She states, "I never wanted to leave it [the farm], but like y' know yourselves the eldest brother—that was our Walter—well he'll always get the farm, and then once he was married there was no more use for me. So I took the wee brothers and sister, just like I promised Mammy I wud, and here we are in Belfast, and thon mill" (I.i). Florrie is a character with whom the audience does not fully identify because she is never again the focus of the narrative; her brief monologue indicates not that she is an individual but rather that her words represent the story of many.

Florrie's monologue, which begins with an assumption of collective understanding, "like y' know yourselves," reminds us that after Britain colonized Ireland in the sixteenth century and through the mid-nineteenth-century famine, women's ability to own property was limited. Although in early Ireland there were provisions for female land ownership, colonization dictated that Ireland must conform to English Common Law: a woman could inherit her father's estate only if there were no sons. When she married, her property reverted to her husband (O'Tuathaigh, 29). In postfamine Ireland, matters became more complicated because marriage was often delayed, and the new Irish state legally permitted women to own property, but land was often willed to a male heir. Charabanc's Florrie must work in the mill to support herself and her younger siblings because of state law, patriarchy, and imperial/capitalist interests, which would, in the early 1900s, still prevent her from owning property.

Ethna McNamara, another spinner, is continually accosted by

the moneylender, a woman who uses the threat of revealing Ethna's delinquency to her husband in order to collect outstanding debts. The moneylender says that if she does not receive what is owed her, she is "goin round nigh to tell your man" (I.ii). The threat is intended to, and does, frighten Ethna. It also indicates the power held by her husband.

Later, we learn that Ethna is indebted, however, in part *because* of her man. One day, as the women enter the mill, they briefly listen as Belle, the initiator of the strike and the woman who the group later learns takes the undesirable part-time job of preparing Belfast's dead for burial, tells of her peculiar form of contraception: "Aye, I don't let him near me . . . I don't let him near me when he's sober" (I.iii). Because birth control is illegal in early-twentieth-century Ireland, Belle uses the only method of reproductive choice available to her. Ethna is unable to do the same and quite literally pays for it: "What do you think has me in debt and danger . . . since my last one was born, in May, I made up my mind, no more childer, eight's enough for any wee girl. But he wudn't hear tell of it" (I.iii). Although after she gives birth to her eighth child the doctor encourages Ethna not to "ly[e] with" her husband, her husband will not hear of it: "Pig, beat me black and blue" (I.iii). Because she wishes to exercise reproductive choice, Ethna is beaten by her husband: "I get it that often, I was thinkin' I might as well go the whole hog and take up professional boxin'" (I.iii).

Ethna's situation, less than the individual Ethna, encourages audiences to react to her lack of reproductive choice and her abusive home. According to Monica McWilliams in "Truth and Fiction in Domestic Violence," domestic violence must be analyzed less in relation to the individual characteristics of either the perpetrator or the victim, and more in terms of the specifically gendered nature of the crime and constructions of gender. Speaking specifically of abuse in Northern Ireland, McWilliams argues that constructions of masculinity permit domestic abuse and that today, by virtue of the specifically masculine/militaristic construction of police and paramilitary organizations, these forces are unavailable to women who are abused (1994a, 5–8). In early-twentieth-century Ireland, Irish Catholic women such as Ethna might have felt unable to contact the Royal Ulster Constabulary, a mostly Protestant police force, regarding domestic abuse; also, these women would have been abused at least partly as a result of the poverty that surrounded them, and also because their husbands were unemployed. Ethna's evocation of reproductive choice and abuse, then, is inextricably bound with the state (the police force) and the political economy (poverty and unemployment), both of which are at least partially the results of colonization.

Lizzie is married to a man named Charlie who makes all his wife's decisions for her and who encourages her not to strike: "A crowd of weemin cannot row a ship Lizzie dear" (I.viii). Charlie's determination that his wife should not strike ultimately manifests itself in his invocation of the cult of motherhood. In what I am referring to as the "cult of motherhood," women are made to think that if they agitate for employment equality, they are putting work concerns before their family. Thus they will be seen as bad mothers. They are not encouraged to go on strike (as their work helps subsidize the family) or to agitate for equality. Charlie orders his wife to cease her foolishness: "Get back til your work in the mornin,' ye can't deprive your wee childer of a bite in ther mouths. . . . [do it] not just for me luv, but for your wee childer and the rest of the weemin in Belfast" (I.viii). Charlie's recourse to the cults of motherhood and domesticity would have received ample support in the next decade, a decade which set the scene for how the Republic and Northern Ireland would continue to view women.

Although Charlie and Lizzie live in what would become the North, decades later, their characters would have been ideologically influenced by the Irish Republic's 1922 and 1937 constitutions. The latter, permanent, constitution encoded women's domestic status in state policy and ensured that a woman's role as domestic being and mother could prohibit her from securing and maintaining employment. As noted earlier in this chapter, in the 1937 constitution women are referred to in the context of the family. Article 41.2 states that "in particular the state recognises that by her life within the home woman gives to the state the support without which the common good cannot be achieved. . . . the state shall therefore endeavour to ensure that mothers shall not be obliged by economic necessity to engage in labour to the neglect of their duties in the home" (quoted in Commission on the Status of Women, *Report to the Second Council,* 23). This article, and the ideology that informs it, has allowed men to use women's role as mothers and homemakers to discourage them from employment; additionally, this ideology has allowed men to discourage women from agitating for equality if they work outside the home. As the article suggests, women are supposed to care more about home than work. Again, this article does not directly affect Charlie and Lizzie because they are portrayed in an earlier time frame and live in Northern Ireland; yet the ethos of the article could nevertheless provide the support Charlie needs. More specifically, Charlie's patriarchal attitudes would have been shared by those who wrote the constitutions.

Mary, the youngest of the group, is about to be married to a man to whom she initially professes great love. Throughout the strike, however, she begins to wonder whether or not she can ever expect equality and happiness with him. Mary says that she "don't want us to end up like themins and their men, fightin' and argun' and hatin' to lie together at night. . . . I know he won't turn into one of them, but how come I got the only good wan?" (II.vi). Although at first Mary is sure of her love, she begins to doubt that it can last. She suggests that other couples fight not as a result of individual personality flaws but rather because of economic hardship. She wonders how her life will be any different if she and her fiancé have lives similar to those of the other women. These monologues are made to stand in for all of the two thousand women who are on strike; the story of Florrie, Lizzie, Mary, Belle, or Ethna could be the story of many others.

The women's grievances throughout the strike are ideological. Belle notes that the women who make the linen cannot afford to buy it, and also that no person should have access to economic profits from the workers' labor when workers themselves do not have enough food to eat. The grievances center on two specific conditions: the women protest the alteration in work hours and the confining and degrading rules imposed upon them. The women were protesting that the hours were shorter (and they would get less pay) and that though the days would be shorter, the week would be longer because they would have to work Saturdays. In an effort to deflect attention from the proposed changes, the mill has erected absurd rules and regulations. With each breakage, the worker is fined. Lizzie reads that "any person found away from their usual place of work, except for necessary purposes; or talkin' with anyone out of their own alley will be fined 2d for each offence. No singin', you're not even allowed to stop to fix your hair" (I.i). The rules demonstrate the unequal relationship between the worker and the mill owner: "All persons in our employ shall serve four weeks notice before leavin' their employ, but E. Bingham and company shall and will dismiss any person without notice being given" (I.i). The rules apply to everyone, not just one laborer; thus the women workers will respond to collective punishment as a group.

When the women do strike, they walk out of the factory together and ultimately seek the advice of two individuals who represent the future options in and for Northern Ireland: socialist James Connolly and Mary Galway, the mill workers' representative. The women visit the Custom House, Belfast's gathering spot, to hear James Connolly speak. Well versed in Marx and Engels, Connolly gives what has become his infamous speech and rallying cry: "The worker is the slave of capitalist society—the female worker is the slave of that slave" (Connolly, 292). Connolly speaks of and about women's inferior status in relation to men on the island of Ireland. Born in Scotland, Connolly once fought for (and then against) the British army; he lectured in North America; and he made his home in Ireland. Remembered today for his fervent loyalty to international socialism, and notwithstanding his, to some, problematic participation in the Easter Rising, Connolly is also heralded for his commitment to women workers. His oft-quoted dictum from *The Re-Conquest of Ireland* is taken as his early warning to the women of Ireland that until they are free, Ireland will remain oppressed. Also significant is Connolly's friendship with the labor leader and women's rights advocate Francis Sheehey-Skeffington.

Although in *Lay Up Your Ends* Connolly does support the

women, in reality, he was often chided for his nationalist sympathies. In the play, Lizzie's husband encourages her to disengage not only from the strike but also from the "home ruler," James Connolly: "Your man Connolly is for the home rule business" (I.viii). Connolly's national allegiances are also taken to task by Mary Galway, who discourages the strike from the beginning and urges the workers back to the mill; she calls Connolly "an extremist and a home ruler" (I.viii). When Connolly's encouragement to the workers begins to have an effect upon them, his national status is questioned.

In the next scene, the spinners, dressed as men, appear as very different characters. They are organized in an ostensibly nonsectarian strike band, reminiscent of the Protestant and Catholic bands organized by Connolly. While Charabanc's decision to cast females in male roles generally demonstrates that Irish women are typically unemployed in the theater, in this instance, the women play the roles of members of a nonsectarian band to symbolize that when we listen to women's voices, we will be closer to achieving a nonsectarian state with fair labor practices.

Although there have been sectarian quips in the play, these two scenes, the scene in which Connolly is labeled a home ruler and the band scene, are the only ones that overtly suggest the tension between labor and nationalism in early-twentieth-century Ireland. These scenes are significant because they are in the minority; their marginal status indicates that although nationalist and unionist tensions were evident in 1911, it was the cause of labor that was most prominent for these women. Regardless of their political allegiance, workers agitated for fair wages and conditions. Significantly, the band scene is the first scene in the second act; in this scene the women collect money for the strike. The audience is led to believe that at the end of the day, although nationalist and unionist tensions exist, for women workers, economic conditions take precedence. Indeed, this move from act I to act II reminds us that the primary focus of the play will remain the cause of labor and *not* the national question.

Yet the sharp disparity between Mary Galway and James Connolly is significant and indicates the tensions within labor in

Northern Ireland. Connolly is the militant Marxist; Galway is a woman who is more interested in slow progress. Her organization is also overtly class conscious. According to one of the spinners, all Galway does is "organise wee clubs for the girls." The spinner notes that Galway "doesn't want to have no truck with the bosses, that's why she steers clear of the spinners, rulers, rovers and doffers—the ordinary mill girls" (I.iv). Although she is often heralded for her efforts as the first female textile organizer, Charabanc argues that Galway's class distinctions exclude the "ordinary mill girls" and do not address their concerns. Galway, too, represents a type rather than simply an individual: she represents labor organizations that neglect ordinary women.

Taken together, Connolly and Galway represent less actual figures in Ireland's labor history and more the divergence of labor in what would become the Republic and Northern Ireland. In 1871 the British Parliament legalized trade union activity and the Irish Trade Union Congress was established in 1894. In the ensuing years, there were problems regarding national allegiances. After World War II, the trade union movement was divided into those who had formed the Congress of Irish Unions and those who stayed loyal to the Irish Trade Union Congress (Boyd, 105). Although the two eventually merged, the status of both in Northern Ireland was fraught with political tensions.

Additionally, women were often not recognized within the unions. According to Mary Daly, in her study of contemporary Ireland, it was not until the 1960s that women began to press for concerns specific to women: namely, equal pay. Until this time, attitudes toward women were hostile; the new Irish state decried women's domestic status; and the general economy was poor. Moreover, both parts of the island were reeling, in different ways, from partition. However, post-1960, women began to gain in public status, to argue for more equitable conditions, and to pave the way for what would become the report on the status of women. These two strands of labor, the question of national allegiance and the status of women, are represented in *Lay Up Your Ends*. As is evident by the increasing electoral support given the Social Democratic Labour Party (SDLP) today, and the emphasis on employment and trade in the peace process, economic and labor concerns are significant in contemporary Northern Ireland. *Lay Up Your Ends* acknowledges that fair labor has been important to women since at least 1911.

Toward the conclusion of the two-week strike, Belle recognizes both the probable cause for "the failure" of the strike and the specifically gendered material difficulty of women workers and protest. She states, "D' ya think I'm wastin m' breath. . . ? It's hard to talk to these weemin about what's right and fair when they've a clatter of starvin weeins at home and maybe their man not workin" (II.vii). It is difficult for women to strike for two reasons: when they do protest, women are perceived to be deviant and less feminine, and women have to worry about material circumstances (starving children and unemployed husbands).

Finally, although their demands have not been met, the women decide to return to work together. Florrie insists: "We're all to gather together, outside the Mill—in a body—and *all* go in singin'" (emphasis in original, II.ix). According to Charabanc, the women become one body as they reenter the work site. In his provocative theorizations of punishment, Foucault has examined the relation between the body and work. His analysis allows us to read the women's decision to reenter the workplace as a body as a signal that their collective resistance will organize itself around the body politic. This collective corporeal solidarity does not cease even after the women reenter the mill. In defiance of company-imposed rules, one of the mill workers blatantly combs her hair, and the others follow suit. Soon, one woman "becomes" (in the sense that one woman resists in the same manner as the other the rules that impose collective punishment) another, and they all comb their hair together. Stage directions indicate that in the final scene, "the women gather centre stage and begin to comb their hair simultaneously" (II.x).

While the women's refusal to adhere to company rules is significant, the fact that they choose to resist this particular rule—no worker shall comb her hair—is paramount. The mill owner previously noted that he imposed this rule because he is sure that women are apt to pay special attention to their hair; thus the women resist a rule that is imposed not just because they are workers but because they are *female* workers. The women, then, react specifically to the gendered nature of their oppression under capitalism; they react to rules imposed upon them strictly because they are females. The women workers' collective resistance does not constitute merely a romanticized view of female solidarity, a solidarity in which women in unrelated circumstances unite in their refusal of patriarchal domination. Rather, in *Lay Up Your Ends*, women in a (post)colonial region unite to resist capitalist oppression in their own work site and on their own terms.

## *Now You're Talkin'*

*Now You're Talkin'* is set in the 1980s and comprises the last play in the trilogy begun by Lynch's drama. Written by Marie Jones and directed by Pam Brighton, the play takes place in a reconciliation center. *Now You're Talkin'* opened in the Belfast Civic Arts Theatre on March 17, 1985, and alludes to the number of reconciliation programs and centers established in the 1980s. It also refers to the Anglo-Irish Agreement (1985), which, among other things, solidified the Republic of Ireland's commitment to Northern Ireland. The term "reconciliation" suggests that the play attempts to reconcile a group of women. Ultimately, however, in one of Charabanc's most biting critiques, the drama illustrates the inadequacy of the concept of reconciliation as it is conceived by multinationalism, the state, paramilitaries, and the media—everybody except women in Northern Ireland.

When Charabanc performed it for the first time in 1985, it stated that the ending was provisional. In fact, the ending changed every couple of weeks of the play's run. According to Marie Jones, because the play was set in contemporary Northern Ireland, "we were frightened of leaving it [the ending] at a moment where people could say, 'Ah, that's what Charabanc thinks, that's a statement'. We invited people we trusted to come and see it and asked them what they thought of the ending. People made different suggestions, and we tried them" (quoted in Martin, 92). This point is important because it demonstrates two things: Charabanc Theatre Company reminds us how difficult it is to create drama out of contemporary political situations, especially when you do not want to be seen to be proscribing an answer; and Charabanc's refusal to come up with a definitive ending mirrors the refusal of *Now You're Talkin'* to privilege one voice.

Unlike *Lay Up Your Ends*, *Now You're Talkin'* begins with a monologue by each woman and moves toward provisional collectivity. Initially, four women arrive at the Atlantic View Reconciliation Center from diverse church and community groups. It is never made clear who owns the center, which is located on prime real estate, but due to the fact that the director of the center is an American, the audience assumes a U.S. presence even if an American company or individual does not literally own the center. Though obviously the name of the reconciliation center is meant to suggest that the land is situated with a view of the ocean and that, therefore, its inhabitants are able to look out beyond Northern Ireland, there are less obvious connotations to the name of the center as well. For some time, the special relationship between the United Kingdom and the United States known as the Atlantic Alliance has rendered American intervention into the plight of Northern Ireland unthinkable to many U.S. politicians. Because the name of the reconciliation center is Atlantic View and because the director is an American, audiences are encouraged to question international intervention into Northern Ireland.

The Atlantic View Reconciliation Center seeks to subsume political differences into a single monolithic identity. For example, Carter O'Donaghue, the center's American director, encourages the group to dance around the maypole. which bears a colored ribbon for each country, and intertwine the ribbons into one. He describes this game as a "quaint old English custom" (I.ii). It never dawns upon him that some women in the group may find an English game that seeks to combine colored ribbons, ribbons which may represent colored flags, offensive. Also, he does not think the women will figure out that he is using the game to urge them to see the benefits of solidarity.

Although the women do not initially speak of their differences, disparate political allegiances do eventually surface. In one reconciliation game Carter suggests that the Northern Irish women free-associate to the word "freedom." One participant, Veronica, notes that for her the word means "freedom for Ireland." There is an awkward silence, and the women later ponder Veronica's disquieting revelation. They perhaps weren't aware that there was a Republican or nationalist in their midst. Charabanc is composed of Catholic and Protestant women who want this diversity to be reflected in their plays. In *Now You're Talkin'* not only do the women hail from diverse cultural backgrounds, but they also inhabit different classes. Veronica gasps when she hears that Thema's coat costs £60, and the spectacle of the diverse backgrounds becomes obvious in another game, a game aimed at erasing or minimalizing differences within the group. Carter explains the "Farmer and the Cowman" as an "Oklahoma custom" in which two groups have territorial feuds but nevertheless "live together in peace and harmony" (I.v). Carter assigns women their roles; as the American mediator, he takes it upon himself to arbitrate feuds and construct alternative groupings, although he is hardly self-reflexive about his country's role in territorial disputes. Thema says she would rather be a cowman, and Carter demurs. Collette does not hesitate to point out why the fixed designations must remain: "'cos they're Protestants i.e. farmers and we're Catholics i.e. cowmen—right?" (I.v). The women have figured out Carter's motives and games.

As Collette notes, these women recognize that they are being categorized, and later they learn about other obvious differences within their group. One latecomer to the group, Madeline, tells the women that she is abused. Carter and the male assistant at the Atlantic View refuse to take her seriously. "Come off it," the assistant says. "A man doesn't bate a woman unless she's done something to annoy him" (I.ii). Carter later asks Madeline if "we are getting over our little domestic crisis" (I.iii). Carter's condescension and his failure to comprehend domestic abuse parallel his inability to fully comprehend the conflict in Northern Ireland. Just as he is complicit in the abuse by not acknowledging its significance, so too has the United States been complicit in the conflict in Northern Ireland by politically acknowledging and attending it belatedly.

Although there is, of course, a large Irish and Irish-American population in the United States, and although there has often been political rhetoric and economic support for the Republic and Northern Ireland from individual U.S. citizens, according to Brendan O'Leary and John McGarry, "before the signing of the Anglo-Irish Agreement in November of 1985 officials in the executive branch of American government usually considered Northern Ireland 'an internal matter' for the government of the UK" (19). Most important, O'Leary and McGarry contend that the Atlantic Alliance, the special relationship between the United Kingdom and the United States "has consistently proved more important for American geopolitical interests than the ethnic sentiments of Irish-Americans" (19). Through the symbols of Carter and the Atlantic View Reconciliation Center, *Now You're Talkin'* alludes to the fact that though individuals and groups in the United States and Britain appear to want to reconcile people in Northern Ireland, for some time, the United States has failed to take action because it does not want to upset its relationship with the United Kingdom. When Carter and the Atlantic View now try to appear as mediator, the effort is redundant: the women know what their needs are, and although they might have welcomed American intervention at one time, Carter and his brand of "help" are now intrusive. I am not suggesting that many people in the Republic and Northern Ireland have not welcomed the assistance today of President Clinton and others. However, Charabanc's play makes it clear that such assistance might have been appreciated earlier, and also that it is accepted graciously when it is offered sincerely and correctly. While I do not have the space to do so here, *Now You're Talkin'* could also be productively read in the context of George Mitchell's role as mediator in the current peace process. How was the intervention of Mitchell, a former senator from the United States, different from that of Carter, and (how) were women's specific needs addressed or not addressed through this intervention?

Although there are individual differences within the group, most of the women agree on collective problems such as economic and gender inequality, and they agree that discussions of the future of Northern Ireland are not taking into consideration their needs. One way the women indicate as much is by resisting Carter, thereby calling into question *his* misunderstanding of reconciliation and community and also his participation in the conflict in the North. Early in the play, Madeline indicates the inadequacy of Carter's idea of maypole togetherness and Oklahoma harmony when she suggests that people should not come together to deny or even ameliorate political differences, because, in the end, it is economic reality that is paramount: "Like, I don't care what yous are, Catholics or Protestants, it's all the same to me. The way I look at it—you can't ate a Union Jack or a Tricolour for yer dinner" (I.ii). Madeline acknowledges that issues of national allegiance are unimportant because they fail to provide material necessities, and during the Maypole dance, Collette notes that the ribbons are not anchored in material reality. She insists that the United States consumes and wastes more food than any other country while elsewhere people are starving. Carter responds that the group isn't discussing "worldly wealth" (I.ii), but the women are unable to divorce worldly wealth from (inter)national inequality: "It's very hard to have peace with your neighbor if you're running about with not a stitch on your back and your neighbor's got a £60 coat" (I.ii).

The women also refuse Carter's essentialist notion of nature, a notion which has implications for economic conditions as well. Carter asks the women to look out to the sea around them: "It is ours to enjoy. Through nature we can find our real selves" (I.i). In contradistinction to contemporary poststructuralist and postmodern theories, Carter not only believes in a "real" self but also imagines that this self can be entirely constructed by an individual, with the help of an idyllic nature. Veronica will not recognize Carter's conception of beauty because her material reality suggests otherwise: "You're dead lucky though, Carter. When I look out my window, I see a dirty great big wall with 'Fuck the UVF' written on it" (I.i). In one fell swoop, this scene questions the individual subject and whether nature can belong to everyone. If, as Carter insists, it is through nature that a woman can find herself, what happens when her access to nature is limited? What happens when she "runs up against a brick wall," one which makes clear the paramilitary presence in her neighborhood? Veronica also subtly points to the difference between a reconciliation center located on prime real estate and her home on the Falls Road.

Veronica's response indicates not the individual subject but rather the construction of women through economic and state considerations. Veronica lives on the Falls Road, and the paramilitary propaganda that surrounds her has everything to do with economics, state and imperial power. Carter's vision of nature, as seen out the windows of the idyllic Atlantic House, is one purchased by a reconciliation group, or by one that has a stake in reconciliation in Northern Ireland. Contrary to what Carter believes, nature and politics cannot be separated.

Finally, the group argues along sectarian and class lines and reveals Carter's complicity in their economic and cultural problems. Veronica and Thema argue about Veronica's lack of money, and when Thema invokes ethnic stereotypes ("what's it to me if yous lot want to breed like rabbits"), the others join the fight. Carter tries to mediate, and one woman screams what she knows Carter does not want to hear: she screams that, yes, the women do indeed hate one another. Carter becomes angry and tells them to leave the center, and the women expose his voyeurism and irresponsible intervention: "You make us expose our inner most feelings and then you ask us to leave" (II.i). Carter can encourage the women to express themselves as long as they say what he wants to hear. Yet the group does not attack Carter as an individual subject; rather, they insist on his construction by the state of his origin: "You Yanks comin over here . . . clear away back to your own country and sort out your own cowboys and Indians!" (II.i). The women remind Carter and the United States that before they tell Northern Ireland what to do, they might contend with their own ethnic conflicts.

In a sign of resistance and collective decision making, the women, in direct opposition to Carter's orders, refuse to vacate the center. Although comprising diverse political, religious, and economic backgrounds, they agree that they must at least be able to disagree without being penalized. To Carter's "Right, you lot, get the fuck out of here," the women respond in unison, "We won't go, we won't go, we won't go" (II.i). When they resist Carter and decide to stay, the women begin to talk among themselves. Indeed, they mock any feminist solidarity that neglects material conditions, "Catholics on the right, Protestants on the left, let's all hold hands and be sisters in love together" (II.i). The women make it clear that they can talk to one another not simply because of their gender; rather, because they are Northern Irish women, they do have certain common concerns. They do not agree on school curricula or the contemporary place of the Irish language, but they do agree on one thing:

Jackie: What I'm sayin' is that there are more important things that we should be concerned about like ending discrimination—religious and sexual.

Madeline: Yes, I'll go along with that, 'cos you see if I was a man, I wouldn't be here—I would've threw him [her abusive husband] out instead. (II.i)

When the women are able to talk among themselves without intervention from what Carter symbolizes—patriarchal interests that stretch across various countries—they agree that while Northern Ireland must contend with "the national question," there are other concerns that are primary to women; ending sexual and religious discrimination, as well as domestic abuse, must be a part of future discussions in the North.

Yet ultimately, their discussion, which acknowledges that they would end the conflict in the North by recognizing shared economic problems, is derailed and interrupted by the media. Unable to visualize the women outside the confines of military strife, the media reports, as the women are agreeing to disagree, that they have "occupied" the center, but that, thus far, there are no signs of arms ("for God's sake," says Madeline, "this is Northern Ireland, if you didn't mention arms you wouldn't get a write-up in the bloody Beano" [II.iv]). The British press interviews the women and attempts (with the help of one of them) to construct the women as female peacemakers. The women refuse to comment on the upcoming summit, which would develop the Anglo-Irish Agreement, and instead focus on the fact that people of Northern Ireland, especially the women of the region, must themselves decide the fate of the region. Their refusal to discuss what would become the Anglo-Irish Agreement is an indication that some women and Protestants were not adequately consulted during negotiations on the agreement and that they have concerns not reflected in the policy. Nevertheless, the reporter essentializes the women and provides a press report that confirms gendered stereotypes. He is all too eager to pick up on one of the woman's assumptions that although this group is not the peace people ("we've got a much more realistic thrust"), females are less violent than males: "I'm sure most of our readers would also agree that the feminine principle is more tolerant, less inclined to violence" (II.vii).

According to Margaret Ward and Marie Theresa McGivern, women protesters and activists in Northern Ireland are often desexed, made deviant, or consigned to the roles of peacemakers by the media: "The media clearly makes its judgment—women who support the status quo, who are fulfilling a traditional caring role—must be treated with kid gloves and admired without criticism. Those who choose other ways are accused of being abnormal—a treatment which is rarely meted out to men. . . . and if their actions do not fit neatly into either category (deviants or peace lovers) then they are ignored" (583).

In the reporter's statement, aired on the radio, the women are heralded for their heroic peace efforts but are also constructed as deviant: "The fifth woman, the most extreme and intransigent of the Catholics has, sadly, refused to cooperate" (II.viii). Actually, the fifth woman is the Republican or nationalist, Veronica. The women tie her up and put her in a closet because they don't want her extremism to ruin their discussions. Others, too, essentialize the women and their efforts. While the women are at the center, the Loyal Defenders paramilitary group delivers a message to them, urging the Protestant women especially to cease "negotiations": "Furthermore, remember your duties, remember your womanhood. What is to become of the future sons of Ulster when their mothers behave in such an unnatural, unwomanly way" (II.vi). The paramilitaries entreat the women to remember their "domestic" place, one not suited to solving state and international problems. Neither the American mediator, the British reporter, nor the Northern Irish paramilitary men can conceive of women outside the cult of domesticity.

According to Susanne Greenhalgh in "The Bomb in the Baby Carriage: Women and Terrorism in Contemporary Drama," women in the theater who are cast as terrorists or activists demonstrate the particularly gendered construction of these roles on stage and in culture: "When women assume the guise of the violent activist, in the theatre or in actuality, this will be most often seen as a form of perverse transvestism, a morbid rejection of her natural role as victim or maternal giver and sustainer of life" (162). The women in *Now You're Talkin'* are portrayed by the media as alternately peace loving and deviant, but by pointing to this construction, Charabanc hopes to begin the process of reversing it.

Ultimately, the women do not agree on the political future of Northern Ireland. Rather, they come to terms with the fact that they all disagree on a great deal. The play does not provide closure for the audience but instead encourages a recognition of difference—a difference which is always constituted by political and economic conditions. This group of women is not, finally, reconciled; yet they agree that they have all been differently constructed by state and economic forces and that whatever the future of Northern Ireland may hold, it must be a future discussed, argued about, and reconfigured by women. In this case, the women represent disparate groups but groups equally concerned about material conditions.

### Somewhere over the Balcony

In the third and final play examined in this chapter, Charabanc takes one specific material condition—internment—and analyses its long-term implications as well as the often ludicrous context of illegal activity and surveillance in Northern Ireland. Written by Marie Jones and directed by Peter Sheridan in 1987, Charabanc's *Somewhere over the Balcony* debuted in London's Drill Hall in September of 1987. The action takes place in August of 1987, the anniversary of the reintroduction of internment. Set in the now-condemned Divis Flats housing estate, the play constructs a group of women, men, and children in order to suggest how the community is alternately created and torn apart by the state. The primary focus on women, the connection with internment, and the setting, in one of the last blocks in the estate to be demolished, all indicate representation or construction within the state and political economy. Additionally, because this is one of Charabanc's least realistic plays, the audience is most obviously encouraged to identify not with specific characters and events but rather with the material construction that comprises these characters and events.

*Somewhere over the Balcony* is replete with individual action and offstage commotion such as helicopter sounds and army truck maneuverings. The action is narrated by the characters but could also be imagined by them; the women remain on stage throughout but take on different guises. At the conclusion of the play, these women revert to their original positions, encouraging us to question the action we have seen and heard. Each action or event, much of which is detailed via the pirate radio broadcasts of one woman, is used to tell us about specific state and/or economic interventions.

The play opens with a spotlight on Kate, who stands with her garbage bin and lid. Our attention is focused on the lid, as Kate is identified by her relation to it: "See this bin . . . thank God for it" (1). Like many other women, in 1972, Kate would have banged the lid to warn the men of Falls Road that the British army was on its way to search and intern them; thus the fact that Kate is initially staged with her bin suggests that she is constructed by its political significance and her relation to the state through it. She is one of the deviant woman who subverted the state by signaling men of approaching danger and she is still defined by this action, just as she has been defined by the injustices she has observed. Yet as noted earlier, the strategy of banging lids was used before internment. In the 1950s, women banged lids to warn their neighborhoods that the rent collectors were coming. Thus, while *Somewhere over the Balcony* is specifically connected to internment, the trope of lid banging must always also remind readers of women's early use of bin lids. Ultimately, their actions signal the material conditions of internment and rent/economic strikes.

Although women here are obviously constructed through state intervention, they also resist and reverse such intervention. In Northern Ireland British soldiers and the RUC often watch people through cameras perched atop buildings; this play subverts this surveillance by demonstrating not only that British soldiers routinely use their camera equipment to survey the people living in the Divis Flats, but also that Kate and her friends watch the soldiers as well. In "State Terror and Dramatic Countermeasures," feminist critic Mary Karen Dahl argues that theater has the potential to resist state oppression of a people by "[using] the texts created by the state in the process of conducting its business as usual to comment on and condemn that business and its associates, who includ[ed] the clergy, the judiciary, the police and other security forces" (114). Thus the women in *Somewhere over the Balcony* use the tools of the state (that is, cameras) to reverse surveillance. The women on the block gaze at the men who have made spectacles of them; they look up at the soldiers through binoculars: "Jesus look at that soldier. . . . they'll be sunbathing up there next. . . . oh he'll be all hot and sweaty now" (3).

According to Trinh T. Minh-ha, colonialist constructions of visibility have everything to do with the West's position as subject of knowledge or as that which acknowledges and constructs what we take to be knowledge. Speaking of the precarious place of the marginal or (post)colonial woman, who is provided scant opportunity to speak or look, Trinh notes that "the postcolonial other is here caught in the regime of visibility as deployed by the West in a wide range of humanistic and anti-humanistic discourses to conserve its leading position as Subject of knowledge" (186). Provocatively, according to Trinh, when she reverses the gaze, the (post)colonial woman still allows the West to be the subject of knowledge; by virtue of the fact that the gaze initiates with the colonizer (his gaze must be reversed), his gaze is primary. Because to merely reverse the gaze is still to provide it with authority (that is, if she merely reverses the gaze, the colonized woman is still taking her cue from and responding to the imperial male), Trinh proposes a displacement of the gaze.

And so Kate and her friends do not merely reverse the soldiers' gazes; they displace them. First, the women use binoculars and thereby remind us of the use of technological warfare (surveillance with machinery) by the British. Next, they look at the men in a manner that men sometimes use to objectify women ("oh he'll be all hot and sweaty"), thus indicating the way women in particular are objectified by regimes of visibility and by the colonial camera. By placing it in another context—their context, the women's home—Charabanc's women reverse the power of the gaze itself. State forces don't own the gaze; women can look, too, and they look from their homes, homes that have previously been surveyed by soldiers.

Just as Kate's relation to her bin and the women's gaze suggest how the women of Divis Flats have been constructed by their relation to state and colonial forces, the audience sees that Kate and her friends are to be taken as constructions within the state and political economy when the women discuss the institution of marriage. When the friends sing of wedding ceremonies (foreshadowing a crucial wedding ceremony later in the play), one woman speaks first, and then another, and then the group speaks in unison: All three marriages could have been one and the same. All of the women were married in a manner that forces a reconsideration of romantic stereotypes and social mythologies, and their words also indicate that the institution of marriage does not help women. Chaos invades what is meant to be a tranquil ceremony:

Ceely: We spend our honeymoon night with him throwin' up in the sink.

Kate: He was on a rebound / It was my mate he wanted instead.

Rose: You'll never want for nothing / That's what my poor Tucker said.

Chorus: For poorer not richer / in sickness not health / it might have been better / to stay on the shelf / good times are coming. Is that what they say / well I'm still here waiting / since my white wedding day. ("The Wedding Song," 13)

Because the women's words merge (in the chorus), and because their stories are similarly disappointing, we are encouraged not to see the women as individual brides but rather as collectively wronged by the marriage contract. What they got was different than what was promised.

"The Wedding Song" foreshadows another scene in the play: the ceremony in which marriage is extricated from the private/domestic realm and placed in the public/political economy. The distinctions between private and domestic, public and political, are questioned. The imaginary wedding farce is narrated by the women, especially by Kate over her pirate radio station. The wedding party is about to be disrupted because the police are looking for a man believed to be in the party. The party refuses to be interrupted and searched, and instead barricades itself in the chapel:

Ceely: They're liftin Tootsie . . . imagine arrestin' a man of the cloth.

Rose: Pack of Heathens.

Kate: Yous will all be struck by lightnin'

Ceely: Shove your walkin' sticks up their. . . .

Rose: Mona is fit to kill; she is beatin' the head of that Paratrooper with her handbag.

Ceely: Charlene! . . . stuff your bouquet down his throat.

Rose: Best dressed riot I ever seen.

Kate: Mona! . . . beat him with your stilettoes. . . .

Ceely: Knock his shite in Father.

Rose: Look at that big pig of a soldier he's throwin' him into the saracen . . . made a lovely wee priest too. (29)

The party's refusal is not an attempt to hide the wanted man (Tootsie dressed as a priest); rather, the guests are trying to resist state intervention. Gayle Rubin's "The Traffic in Women: Notes on the 'Political Economy' of Sex" examines how females are exchanged for use by patriarchal capitalism in the wedding ceremony: "Marriage transactions—the gifts and material that circulate in the ceremonies marking a marriage—are a rich source of data for determining exactly who has which rights in whom" (87). Charabanc's play extends this analysis to indicate that (post)colonial women might contend not only with patriarchal capitalism in the form of the traffic (exchange) of women but also with state interference into what is hailed as a private affair. Both Rubin's essay and Charabanc's play provide further evidence that the wedding ceremony is a public event with public repercussions; it is not the private, romantic event Kate and her friends have been led to believe. Additionally, as Kate and her friends' chorus suggests, the ceremony is sometimes followed by material deprivation.

When they finally do arrest some of the wedding party, the police also lift, or question, Rose. The soldiers use Rose to get to her husband: "We know your twins throw stones at us. Who taught them to do that . . . your husband?" (37). When the soldiers interrogate Rose, they speak in terms of her motherhood: "What would happen them two wee boys if we were to arrest your husband as well . . . put them in an orphanage?" (43). The state uses the ideology of motherhood to torment this young woman, and, as was discussed in chapter 3, the method of interrogating a young woman is specifically gendered.

Yet ultimately, the play's action cannot be resolved; indeed, resolution is not on the agenda. In the penultimate scene, Granda Tucker, who has not spoken since internment, hijacks an army helicopter and moves to free the wedding party that is barricaded in the chapel. In the final scene, things are back to normal, and the women are looking forward to observing the wedding. It is not clear whether or not the incidents described have actually occurred; nor do audience members really know who the women are. We are not sure if they represent the same women we heard from throughout the play or not; we can only place them as representatives of groups of women. The audience is not allowed to see the resolution of events; rather, it is left only with questions.

If we rely on the definition postulated by Mary Karen Dahl, we can discern that Charabanc uses the texts created by the state to condemn that entity. Charabanc's *Somewhere over the Balcony* uses the texts created by the state—Divis Flats, surveillance, institutionalized marriage, and state machinery and technology such as helicopters and binoculars—to comment on and condemn women's construction by the state and political economy.

Although it is explicitly concerned with a feminist agenda, Charabanc has defined itself as working-class theater, thereby insisting on the primacy of material conditions. The company examines women's collective material concerns to demonstrate that such an examination is required if a different Northern Ireland is to be imagined. In the next, and final, section of this book, some women's solutions to their material concerns are discussed.

# Women and a

# Lasting Peace in

# Northern Ireland

As each of the preceding chapters suggests, although nationalist and Republican women recognize and work toward a resolution to the conflict in Northern Ireland, many do not name the troubles as their only concern. Indeed, many women recognize that their lives will remain substantially unchanged after "the war" unless their material needs are considered now. While women's concerns are diverse, they encompass domestic abuse, unemployment, poverty, and inadequate housing as well as what are considered the broader political issues. Their economic and cultural conditions often come to the forefront when we discuss incarceration, because imprisonment illustrates and often exacerbates the tension between women's needs and their oppression by state and (post)-colonial forces as well as by Republicanism and nationalism.

Certainly, when they talk about peace, women insist that there must be some resolution (inter)nationally; yet they do not necessarily believe that a United Ireland or a Northern Ireland state alone will solve their problems. Thus they recognize that any peace that fails to consider specifically gendered and material conditions will not necessarily ensure a better life for all. Many women argue that the peace negotiations must consider not only the future governance of the North but also employment, education, housing, violence against women, and the fate of those who are imprisoned and their families. Just as they call for a broader discussion of what it means, many women accept that different people have diverse agendas for peace. Some argue that peace negotiations must center on a cessation of violence on all sides (including on the part of the state and against women) and must also set the stage for a future in which women are given leadership roles. Others insist that women need the skills that would allow them to participate in a changing Northern Ireland, one less dependent on British subvention and more reliant on cross-border trade. Still others urge a recognition of women's involvement in political parties and community groups; these women note that in part because of the troubles, women have become outspoken activists and should therefore be present at any bargaining table.

Because I do not have the space to delineate all of their needs, and because not all women have publicly discussed or written about their concerns, my suggestions here will be necessarily incomplete. However, because they recognize that certain opportunities will be more significant than others, some women agree that the following mechanisms *may* offer them equality in the future: the Northern Ireland Women's Coalition (NIWC) and women's participation in the peace talks, a constitution, trade unions, the European Union, the women's movement, and community groups. As many reports about the future of Northern Ireland indicate, the issue of prisoners is a significant one. Women have contributed to that discussion as well.

### Incarceration

There has been much talk about the significance of prisoners for the peace talks. According to prisoners' rights activist Mairead U. Adhmaill, "It is widely acknowledged that the ceasefires would not have come about without the say-so of the prisoners and to continue to treat these men and women as the British Government has is to ignore their influence within the Republican Movement and within the wider Republican/nationalist community" (30). Adhmaill notes that in 1996, conditions for prisoners became worse and that of those released on goodwill efforts, one half were due to be released anyway. Twenty-six Irish prisoners remain in high-security prisons throughout England; of these, ten men have served over twenty years (30). The Republic of Ireland's slow ratification of the European Convention on the Transfer of Sentenced Prisoners contributed to the problem as well (30–31). Interestingly, Adhmaill only mentions men and women who are incarcerated; she does not attend to the details of women's experience in prison or how families and the economy of Northern Ireland will be altered after prisoners are released.

Though only time will tell the effect of incarceration on the future of Northern Ireland, one wonders what difference the experience of imprisonment will have on culture. Will males who have been incarcerated be more sensitive to the needs and roles of women if they have been educated about feminism in prison? Will formerly incarcerated women work to recognize and improve the conditions they find outside prison, just as they fought to highlight inadequate conditions inside the institution? How will people become employed? What understanding of democracy will former prisoners bring to a new region?

As I write this in July of 1998, the issue of prisoners remains one of Sinn Fein and the Republican movement's chief negotiating points: they have agreed to continue to uphold the ceasefire and to discuss peace as long as prisoners are released. Incarceration, then, is one of the most significant material conditions involved in the peace process. However, it is not just the Republican movement that is concerned. Sanctioned political parties in Northern Ireland also recognize the importance of this issue. According to Eilish Rooney, the newly formulated NIWC "took a progressive stance in opposing conditional admissions to talks, on prisoners, the criminal justice system, and the Royal Ulster Constabulary" (1997, 548). While the NIWC sees its task as that of getting women heard, and although it recognizes that to do so it must tread lightly on certain issues because the coalition is composed of people from various political allegiances, it nevertheless felt it significant to address the issue of prisoners.

## The Northern Ireland Women's Coalition

In its "Manifesto Election Communication" (1996), the NIWC states that its goal is to "get at least two women to all party talks" (1). The women in the coalition want to raise the profile of women in politics in Northern Ireland and to highlight the contribution women have made to society and can make to political progress (2). Theirs is a cross-community coalition that includes women from all walks of life and political affiliations. The coalition recognizes that while women have been involved in politics with what it terms a "small p," they need to proceed farther. The coalition also maintains that it is simply not true, as some people believe, that because women are not internationally visible in the peace process, they are not politically active in the North (2). Women have long been involved in party politics, community groups, women's movements, and adult education (McWilliams and Kilmurray).

The coalition recognizes, too, what it sees as the three major forces that raised the issue of women and politics: the election of Mary Robinson and her desire to see cross-cultural and community links, the emphasis on women and decision making at the European Union Fourth Medium-Term Action Programme, 1995–96, and the participation of Irish women in the UN Fourth World Conference on Women, Beijing, 1995 (McWilliams and Kilmurray, 17).

The NIWC did win two seats to the all party talks in 1996. In the Northern Ireland forum elections, the NIWC received 7,731 votes, or 1 percent of the total, and sent Monica McWilliams and Pearl Sugar to the talks (Rooney 1997, 548). Ultimately, the coalition has stood for gender equality and an inclusive peace process. According to Monica McWilliams and Avila Kilmurray, "The Coalition's view is that this culture [the culture of mainstream politics in Northern Ireland] may not change until representative democracy becomes more fully inclusive of women" (20). The group plans to work with a wide spectrum of women to address the specific concerns of all women in Northern Ireland.

## Community Groups

The NIWC recognizes what Mary Robinson's support of community groups has meant for women in Northern Ireland. In recent years women in the Republic and the North have made significant gains by participating in such groups. In the Republic community groups have often focused on women's writing, education, activism, and more broadly defined material issues such as housing estate repairs, for example. In *The Hidden Tradition: Feminism, Women, and Nationalism in Ireland,* Carol Coulter views women's community groups as one of the major possibilities for women on the entire island of Ireland. As evidence for this view, she cites former president Mary Robinson's public support of the groups. Coulter notes that "throughout both rural and urban Ireland, especially in the most deprived areas, women's groups have sprung up, devoted to personal and community development, tackling a wide range of problems" (1993, 51). Women have grouped together to form tenant associations, to discuss educational opportunities, and to write.

In Northern Ireland, some of these groups include women of all political persuasions; those groups that are not politically inclusive have begun to educate themselves about different cultures and groups. Coulter does not mention that some groups are finding that the funding available to them in Northern Ireland is for cross-cultural work only (Rooney 1997, 546). Coulter argues that women's community groups have been organized as the result of several factors: the women's movement, an increased number of women in employment outside the home, the greater availability of contraception, "growing problems" such as drug abuse and increased urbanization, and, most urgently, "a disillusionment with central government, established institutions, and political parties" (1993, 51). Coulter analyzes, too, the peculiar growth of women's groups in Northern nationalist enclaves. She calls attention to the contradiction inherent in women's groups that seek to move away from a centralized and alienating government and toward a nationalist ideology that seeks to overthrow one state in order to replace it with another. She ultimately decides that this contradiction suggests that women "are expressing themselves within their different cultures, while adapting and reinterpreting them" (1993, 55). Women, especially women in Northern Ireland, are "expressing themselves," but they are also uniting as a result of the failure of the state to recognize their needs. While Coulter is optimistic, Eilish Rooney's research suggests that community groups have been a powerful force for change, but that unless these groups receive adequate funding, they will not prosper. Rooney notes that in Northern Ireland, "there is no sense of a coherent overall funding or support strategy to consolidate the activities of local women's groups or to aid women in their community participation" (1997, 546). She argues too that "the absence of any coherent strategy for aiding women's participation at community level in NI may have adverse consequences for vital but vulnerable developments" (546).

### The Women's Movement and Inclusion

Because this book has dealt extensively with the theory and practice of the women's movement in Northern Ireland, it will not be discussed in detail here. Suffice it to say that in part because of the difficulty feminists had reaching consensus on incarceration and what were often considered the broader political issues, the Northern Irish women's movement has found it hard to sustain itself. However, many women still believe the movement has the potential to be a catalyst for change in Northern Ireland. Most recognize that to be effective, the women's movement must strive to include women from diverse backgrounds, cultures, and political beliefs.

In "Women in Political Conflict," Eilish Rooney admits that "I feel, and choose to believe, that the demands that women are making to be heard will have an impact. If I examine the history of women's efforts to be included in new structures, even in debates about new structures, then, despite the hard work and the proposals, I have to conclude that women will be ignored" (1995b, 52). Rooney has hope and faces reality; she also believes that when women truly recognize difference, they can make progress. "The commonalties and the differences in women's interests, experiences and oppressions are embedded within those hierarchies [class, age, sexuality]. No serious engagement in political debate, and in the formation of tactical political alliances, can make fundamental political progress without these recognitions" (53). While Rooney may initially feel pessimistic about how women's contributions are received, she does recognize that women have been a powerful force for change in Northern Ireland. She simply does not think this will continue unless nationalist and Unionist, Protestant and Catholic, and middle- and working-class women work together. She wants women to recognize Protestant women's specific relation to Protestant men and to consider whether and how women have had access to power. Yet she states firmly that even this may not be enough; all women must learn to build coalitions based on "economic injustice" (54). Only then will her skepticism be alleviated.

## The European Union and the Trade Union Movement

Some women believe that Northern Ireland's membership in the European Union also has the potential to assist them. Others remain cautious, however. Sylvia Meaney, a former chair of the Employment and Equality Agency in the Republic and a trade unionist, has argued that "equal rights in a non-equal situation do nothing for women" (Meaney 1993). When I heard her speak in 1993, Meaney said she deplored the former and ongoing discrimination directed at women in the workforce in the Republic of Ireland, and that the government's role as a member state in the EU has the *potential* to make such blatant discrimination more difficult for the state. Yet she also recognized the problematics of EU membership. This tension is demonstrated in Northern Ireland by the intervention of the European Court thus far; the court has helped encourage diversity and tolerance on one level, and not helped on another. In 1982, the court decriminalized homosexuality; yet, due to religious and political pressures, abortion is still illegal in the North, and for a time, the EU did not intervene (McWilliams 1991, 82–83). Additionally, although in the past the High Court of Ireland made it legal for clinics and doctors to provide abortion information under the right to travel, the EU recognized the Republic's "special status" and allowed it to enact its own abortion laws. Thus the EU has not always acted in the service of women.

In *Women in Ireland: The Impact of 1992,* Hazel Morrissey recognizes the potential in European Union membership but also cautions that there is much to be done to safeguard working women's rights. Morrissey notes that "the Single European Act [1992] thus offers contradictory possibilities. On the one hand it increases monopolization and the underdevelopment of the peripheries while on the other it will offer significant opportunities to engage in new forms of politics at the European level" (23). Morrissey's research indicates that because the birthrate is declining, Irish women will have more opportunities to enter the workforce but that younger, better-educated women will benefit most from EU membership; older, less-skilled women will gain little (9). According to Morrissey, because a significant number of women who do work in Northern Ireland are in manufacturing jobs dealing with clothing, food, drink, and tobacco, they stand to lose as these industries become more vulnerable to liquidation and absorption. Women also comprise a large portion of the service sector, which includes occupations with variable status and earning power. Morrissey thinks public sector workers will fare well from the EU, just as they have from British subvention in Northern Ireland. Yet a decrease in British subvention will mean a decrease in public sector jobs. Additionally, new cross-border trading and investment could offer employment opportunities, but unless they have proper training, women will not be able to avail themselves of these opportunities. In the future, Northern Ireland's greater participation in the EU and cross-border trade will increase the need for skilled laborers and managers. Women might also need to create more crèche facilities and provide for child care outside the home. Northern Ireland is still a region that depends to a significant extent on mothers in the home and on an extended family network of women. Thus the postreconciliation role of the EU could help but might also harm women.

On another note, although it has had many upsets and although its historical treatment of women has been complicated, many contend that the Northern Ireland trade union movement has the potential to help women (Morrissey). In addition, many female trade unionists are involved in the women's movement and are concerned with the intersection of class and gender. There are now women trade unionists who are involved in the Northern Ireland Women's Coalition. According to Chris Hudson, the Northern Irish Trade Union Congress suggests both the potential and the problematic of women's participation in trade union activity. Hudson notes that although the trade unions fought for and secured legislation on equal pay, sexual harassment in the workforce, and maternity leave, trade unions themselves still reflect women's unequal status in society: while there are many female trade unionists, there are few women in official or executive positions (Hudson, 34). However, women can use their position in the trade union movement to be alert to employment changes in a newly reconfigured Northern Ireland and to agitate for gender equality in cross-border trade and economy. Women in the trade union movement can begin now to press for fair employment and higher wages in a differently constructed region. They can also work to increase awareness of the job-skills training women will need to be competitive. Finally, as some already do, they can bring their skills to the women's movement in order to increase the focus on women and employment in/equality.

## A (New) Constitution?

Many scholars agree that whatever the future of Northern Ireland, attention must be paid to the region's constitution. Unlike Britain, which does not have a written constitution, the North has an articulated statement, though not a bill of rights. Theoretically, the constitution guarantees some rights to all people in the region. Northern Ireland has had a written constitution since it was created by the Government of Ireland Act of 1920. The North's constitution establishes a bicameral Northern Ireland Parliament, originally elected by a system of proportional representation; Westminister is the major body of control, and there is limited cross-border (North-South) relations. In 1972, direct rule ushered in another phase of the constitution. The 1973 act abolished the Northern Ireland Parliament and included a constitutional guarantee of majority consent. Later, provisions were made for devolution and cross-community consensus (through the Sunningdale Agreement and the Anglo-Irish Agreement). Importantly, on December 15, 1993, John Major, then prime minister of Britain and Albert Reynolds, then taoiseach, or prime minister, of Ireland, issued the Downing Street Declaration. Specifically, the document states that Britain has "no selfish strategic or economic interest in Northern Ireland." Reynolds said that it would be wrong to impose a united Ireland unless a majority of the people of Northern Ireland wanted it. Most recently, in 1998, the Republic voted overwhelmingly to do away with its constitutional claim to Northern Ireland.

Scholars have suggested that the problem with the current constitution is that it substantially fails to guarantee rights (for example, freedom from religious and political discrimination is mandated, but there are no provisions for other kinds of discrimination). The inclusion of the Anglo-Irish Agreement institutionalizes an acknowledgment of two communities, thus failing to recognize the differences within communities and the multiplicity of communities in the region. Finally, the constitution's failure to address gender is particularly relevant in light of the Republic of Ireland's 1937 constitution and the impact that has had on women. This failure to account for a woman's individual rights has constructed her as secondary to the fetus and has also allowed employment discrimination. Thus, while a new constitution has the potential to assist women in the North, such a document has not always helped women.

According to many women in Northern Ireland, that which is currently being heralded as the peace process, and that which has the potential to reconfigure this region, is often publicly articulated by men. Women's needs, specifically their material needs, are not being adequately addressed.

However, women insist that there are structures that *may* help them better articulate their needs and more fully participate in what could be a different form of government and a reconfigured region. The Northern Ireland Women's Coalition is a potentially liberating force for women, as is the women's movement. Along with a more just constitution, a more vocal and equitable European Union and a vital trade union movement have the potential to help women. Community groups that recognize and learn from all people in the North have been and no doubt will continue to be productive. Also, it has been acknowledged that throughout the troubles women have been involved in local and grassroots discussions and planning; the skills they learned during this time could help them become involved in a new Northern Ireland.

Understandably, however, women are cautious, and they do not agree on whether or not the structures outlined above will ultimately benefit them. For example, some people believe that until education is fully integrated, divided communities will remain the norm. But many women do agree on one thing: their economic and cultural needs must be considered before peace can become a real possibility. Long doubly oppressed by state and colonial forces along with patriarchy, they recognize what it is like to be silenced and neglected by politics. Yet in their fiction, nonfiction, film, and theater, women demonstrate that "at the end of the day," the future of Northern Ireland will remain substantially unaltered if their needs and material conditions are not recognized in the present. Fortunately for us, women have cogently and astutely articulated these needs and conditions. What we have to do now is listen.

Ackroyd, Carol. 1997. *The Technology of Political Control.* Harmonds-
worth: Penguin.

Adams, Gerry. *Cage Eleven.* 1990. Dingle, Co. Kerry: Brandon.

Adhmaill, Mairead U. 1996. "A Recipe for Disaster: The Place of Prisoners in the Peace Process." *Irish Reporter* (Dublin) 21 (February): 29–33.

Beckett, Mary. 1980. *A Belfast Woman.* New York: William Morrow.

———. 1987. *Give Them Stones.* London: Bloomsbury.

Bell, Desmond. 1991. "Cultural Studies in Ireland and the Postmodernist
Debate." *Irish Journal of Sociology* 1: 83–95.

Borrill, Rachel. 1997. "Motion Seeks McAliskey Treatment Review." *Irish
Times* (Dublin), February 11.

Boyd, Andrew. 1972. *The Rise of the Irish Trade Unions, 1729–1970.* Tralee,
Co. Kerry: Anvil Books.

Britain and Ireland Human Rights Centre. 1997. "Roisin McAliskey:
A Briefing Paper." Free Roisin McAliskey Web site: http://lark-
spirit.com/Roisin. Paper prepared February 29.

Campbell, Brian, et al. 1994. *Nor Meekly Serve My Time: The H Block
Struggle, 1976–1981.* Belfast: Beyond the Pale Publications.

*The Captive Voice: An Glor Gafa.* 1990. Editorial. Vol. 2, no. 2, summer.
Published by the POW Department of Sinn Fein.

Carlen, Pat. 1983. *Women's Imprisonment: A Study in Social Control.* London, Boston, Melbourne, and Henley: Routledge and Kegan Paul.

Charabanc Theatre Company. Carol Moore, artistic director. 1983. *Lay Up Your Ends*, by Martin Lynch and Charabanc Theatre Company, Belfast. Unpublished play. Dir. Pam Brighton.

———. 1985. *Now You're Talkin'*, by Marie Jones, Belfast. Unpublished play. Dir. Pam Brighton.

———. 1987. *Somewhere over the Balcony*, by Marie Jones, Belfast. Unpublished play. Dir. Peter Sheridan.

———. 1995. Correspondence with the author. April 5.

———. N.d. *Charabanc Theatre Company*. Belfast: Charabanc.

Commission on the Status of Women. 1993. "Constitution and Legal Issues." In *Report to the Second Council*, 23. Dublin.

Connolly, James. 1917. *The Re-Conquest of Ireland*. Dublin: Maunsel.

Connolly, John. 1997. "SPUC Intervenes on Behalf of McAliskey." *Irish Times* (Dublin), February 17.

*Constitution of the Republic of Ireland*, article 40.3.3. 29.

Coulter, Carol. 1991. *Web of Punishment: An Investigation*. Dublin: Attic Press.

———. 1993. *The Hidden Tradition: Feminism, Women, and Nationalism in Ireland*. Cork: Cork University Press.

Craig, Sandy. 1980. *Dreams and Deconstructions: Alternative Theatre in Britain*. Derbyshire: Amber Lane Press.

Crilly, Anne, dir. 1988. *Mother Ireland*. Derry: Derry Film and Video.

———. 1991. "Banning History." *History Workshop Journal*, 163–65.

———. 1994. Interview by author. Dublin, March 9.

Cullen, Kevin. 1995. "Prisoner Issue Takes Center Stage in Ulster." *Boston Globe,* July 9.

Cullen, Luke. 1968. *The Anne Devlin Jail Journal*. Cork: Mercier Press.

Dahl, Mary Karen. 1990. "State Terror and Dramatic Countermeasures." In *Terrorism and Modern Drama*, ed. John Orr and Dragan Klaic, 109–21. Edinburgh: Edinburgh University Press.

Daly, Mary. 1989. *Women and Poverty*. Dublin: Attic Press.

D'Arcy, Margaretta. 1981. *Tell Them Everything: A Sojourn in the Prison of Her Majesty Queen Elizabeth at Ard Macha (Armagh)*. London: Pluto Press.

Devlin, Bernadette. 1969. *The Price of My Soul*. New York: Knopf.

DiCenzo, Maria. 1993. "Charabanc Theatre Company: Placing Women Center-Stage in Northern Ireland." *Theatre Journal* 45: 174–84.

Edgerton, Lynda. 1986. "Public Protest, Domestic Acquiescence: Women in Northern Ireland." In *Caught Up in the Conflict: Women's Response to*

*Political Strife,* ed. Rosemary Ridd and Helen Callaway, 71–76. London: Macmillan.

Emerman, Marsha. 1989. "Film, Video, and Self-Representation in Northern Ireland." *Cineaste* 17, no. 2: 40–41.

Engels, Friedrich. [1884] 1946. *The Origin of the Family, Private Property, and the State.* London: Lawrence and Wishart.

Evason, Eileen. 1991. *Against the Grain: The Contemporary Women's Movement in Northern Ireland.* Dublin: Attic Press.

Ford, Richard. 1991. "McAliskey to Keep Baby with Her in Jail for 9 Months." *London Times,* March 14.

Foster, John. 1976. "British Imperialism and the Labour Aristocracy." In *The General Strike: 1926,* ed. John Skelley, 3–57. London: Lawrence and Wishart.

Foster, John Wilson. 1991. *Colonial Consequences: Essays in Irish Literature and Culture.* Dublin: Lilliput Press.

Foucault, Michel. 1977. *Discipline and Punish: The Birth of the Prison,* trans. Alan Sheridan. New York: Pantheon.

———. 1991. *Remarks on Marx: Conversations with Duccio Trombadori.* New York: Simeotext(e).

Gibbons, Luke. 1982–84. "To Tell the Truth: *Maeve,* History, and Irish Cinema." *The Crane Bag* 6–8: 148–55.

Gormally, Brian, ed. 1990. "The Visiting Experience." In *Silent Sentence: Working with Prisoners' Families,* 8–13. Report and Guidelines to Practice Arising from the NIACRO International Conference, October 29 and 30. Belfast: Information Unit, NIACRO.

Greenhalgh, Susanne. 1990. "The Bomb in the Babycarriage: Women and Terrorism in Contemporary Drama." In *Terrorism and Modern Drama,* ed. John Orr and Dragan Klaic, 160–83. Edinburgh: Edinburgh University Press.

Hackett, Claire, and Maire Quiery. 1994. "Sisterhoods Are Powerful: Acknowledging the Different Identities of Women." *Irish Reporter* 16 (fourth quarter): 16–18.

Harkin, Margo, dir. 1989. *Hush-A-Bye Baby.* Derry: Derry Film and Video.

———. 1991. Symposium speaker. In *Culture, Identity, and Broadcasting in Ireland: Local Issues, Global Perspectives,* ed. Martin McLoone, 110–16, and 134 ("Discussion"). Proceedings of the Cultural Traditions Group/Media Studies, U.U.C. Symposium. Belfast: Institute of Irish Studies, Queens University.

Harkin, Margo, and Tom Collins. 1989. "Synopsis, *Hush-A-Bye Baby*." Derry.

Harlow, Barbara. 1992. *Barred: Women, Writing, and Political Detention*. Hanover and London: Wesleyan University Press.

Headrick, Charlotte. 1998. "'Moving a Mountain with a Spoon': The Circle Is Unbroken. Personal Narratives into Political Drama: Charabanc's *Lay Up Your Ends*." Unpublished Paper. American Conference for Irish Studies, Fort Lauderdale.

Hennessey, Rosemary, and Rajeswari Mohan. 1989. "The Construction of Woman in Three Popular Texts of Empire: Towards a Critique of Materialist Feminism." *Textual Practice* 3, no. 3 (winter): 323–59.

Hudson, Chris. 1994. "Through Thick and Thin." *Fortnight: An Independent Review of Politics and the Arts* 328 (May): 34–35.

Independent Film, Video and Photography Association. 1988. *Fast Forward: Report on the Funding of Grant-Aided Film and Video in Northern Ireland*. Northern Ireland: Independent Film, Video and Photography Association.

*Irish Times* (Dublin), May 1995.

Jennings, Anthony, et al. 1988. *Justice under Fire: The Abuse of Civil Liberties in Northern Ireland*. London: Pluto Press.

Johnston, Claire. 1981. "*Maeve*: An Interview with Pat Murphy." *Screen* 4: 54–71.

Kelly, Frieda. 1988. *A History of Kilmainham Gaol: The Dismal House of Little Ease*. Cork and Dublin: Mercier.

Kilmurray, Avila. 1987. "Women in the Community in Northern Ireland: Struggling for Their Half of the Sky." *Studies* 76, no. 302 (summer): 177–84.

Kristeva, Jula. 1986. *The Kristeva Reader*, ed. Toril Moi. New York: Columbia University Press.

Lacan, Jaques. 1977. *The Four Fundamental Concepts of Psycho- Analysis*, trans. Alan Sheridan. London and New York: Norton.

Lloyd, David. 1993. *Anomalous States: Irish Writing and the Post- Colonial Moment*. Durham: Duke University Press.

Longley, Edna. 1994. "From Cathleen to Anorexia: The Breakdown of Irelands." In *A Dozen Lips*, 162–87. Dublin: Attic Press.

Luddy, Maria, and Cliona Murphy. 1989. *Women Surviving*. Dublin: Poolbeg.

Lyons, Laura E. 1992. "'At the End of the Day': An Interview with Mairead Keane, National Head of Sinn Fein Women's Department." *boundary 2* 19, no. 2: 260–86.

Marron, Oonagh. 1994. "Women's Agenda for Peace." In *Clar na mBan Conference Report,* 9. Belfast: Clar na mBan Publication.

Martin, Carol. 1977. "Charabanc Theatre Company: 'Quare' Women 'Sleggin' and 'Geggin' the Standards of Northern Ireland by 'Tappin' the People." *Drama Review* 31, no. 2 (summer): 88–99.

Marx, Karl. 1906. *Capital: A Critique of Political Economy,* trans. Samuel Moore and Edward Aveling. New York: Modern Library.

Marx, Karl, and Frederick Engels. [1939] 1970. *The German Ideology.* New York: International Publishers.

McAliskey, Bernadette Devlin. 1997. "Roisin McAliskey's Alibi, Interview with Bernadette Devlin McAliskey." Interviewed by Sandy Boyer and Brian Mor, August 16. Dublin: RTE.

McAliskey, Roisin. 1998. "Open Letter." March. Free Roisin McAliskey Web site: http://larkspirit.com/Roisin.

McCafferty, Nell. 1985. "Virgin on the Rocks." In *Seeing Is Believing: Moving Statues in Ireland,* ed. Colm Toibin, 53–58. Mountrath, Co. Laois: Pilgrim Press.

———. 1994. "It Is My Belief That Armagh Is a Feminist Issue." In Kate Donovan et al., *Ireland's Women: Writings Past and Present,* 19–22. Dublin: Gill and Macmillan.

McKeown, Lawrence. 1990. "The Visit." *The Captive Voice: An Glor Gafa* 2 no. 2 (summer): 10.

McLoone, Martin. 1993. "A Little Local Difficulty?: Public Service Broadcasting, Regional Identity, and Northern Ireland." In *The Regions, the Nations, and the BBC,* ed. Sylvia Harvey and Kevin Robbins, 38–48. London: British Film Institute, BBC Charter Review Series.

McWilliams, Monica. 1991. "Women in Northern Ireland: An Overview." In *Culture and Politics in Northern Ireland, 1960–1990,* ed. Eamonn Hughes, 81–100. Milton Keynes and Philadelphia: Open University Press.

———. 1993. "The Church, the State, and the Women's Movement in Northern Ireland." In *Irish Women's Studies Reader,* ed. Ailbhe Smyth, 79–100. Dublin: Attic Press.

———. 1994a. "Truth and Fiction in Domestic Violence." *Irish Reporter* (Dublin) 14 (second quarter): 5–8.

———. 1994b. "The Woman 'Other.'" *Fortnight: An Independent Review of Politics and the Arts* 328 (May): 24–25.

———. 1995. "Struggling for Peace and Justice: Reflections on Women's Activism in Northern Ireland. *Journal of Women's History* 6, no. 4 and 7, no. 1 (winter–spring): 13–39.

McWilliams, Monica, and Avila Kilmurray. 1997. "Athene on the Loose, the Origins of the Northern Ireland's Women's Coalition." *Irish Journal of Feminist Studies* 2, no. 1 (summer): 1–21.

Meaney, Gerardine. 1994. "Sex and Nation: Women in Irish Culture and Politics." In *A Dozen Lips,* 188–204. Dublin: Attic Press.

Meaney, Sylvia. 1993. "Irish Women and the EU." Women's Studies Lecture. University of Rhode Island, February 3.

Mitchell, Juliet. 1971. *Woman's Estate.* New York: Pantheon.

Morrissey, Hazel. 1989. *Women in Ireland: The Impact of 1992.* Belfast: Amalgamated Transport and General Workers Union.

Mulvey, Laura. 1988. "Visual Pleasure and Narrative Cinema." In *Feminism and Film Theory,* ed. Constance Penley, 57–68. New York: Routledge; London: British Film Institute.

———. 1989. "British Feminist Film Theory's Female Spectators: Presence and Absence." *Camera Obscura: A Journal of Feminism, Culture, and Media* 20, no. 21 (September): 68–81.

Murphy, Pat. 1982. "Open Letter," April 7.

———, dir. 1984. *Anne Devlin.* London: British Film Institute.

———. 1994. Interview by the author, April.

Murphy, Pat, and John Davis, dirs. 1981. *Maeve.* London: British Film Institute with Radio Telefis Eireann.

Murphy, Patsy. 1982. "Maeve." *IFS News* 5, no. 4 (April): 8–10.

———. 1990. "Hush-A-Bye Baby." *Film Base News* (February–March): 8–11.

Newton, Judith, and Deborah Rosenfelt. 1985. *Feminist Criticism and Social Change: Sex, Class, and Race in Literature and Culture.* New York: Methuen.

Nic Giolla Easpaig (Gillespie), Aine, and Eibhlin Nic Giolla Easpaig. 1987. *Sisters in Cells: Two Republican Prisoners in England.* Trans. Nollaig O Gadhra. Westport, Co. Mayo: Foilseachain Naisiunta Teoranta.

Northern Ireland Women's Coalition. 1996. "Northern Ireland Women's Coalition, Manifesto Election Communication." *Irish Journal of Feminist Studies* 1, no. 2 (winter): 1–2.

Nutt, Kathleen. 1993. "Beyond Women in Green: Some Remarks on Irish Feminist Films." Unpublished Paper. Imagining Ireland Conference: A Weekend of Discussion, Culture, and Politics. Irish Film Institute, October 29–31.

O'Dowd, Liam. 1989. "Neglecting the Material Dimension: Irish Intellectuals and the Problem of Identity." *Irish Review* 3: 8–17.

———. 1991. "The States of Ireland: Some Reflection on Research." *Irish Journal of Sociology* 1: 96–106.

———. 1994. *Whither the Irish Border?: Sovereignty, Democracy, and Economic Integration in Ireland.* Belfast: Center for Research and Documentation Publications.

O'Leary, Brendan, and John McGarry. 1993. *The Politics of Antagonism: Understanding Northern Ireland.* London and Atlantic Highlands: Athlone Press.

O'Sullivan, Kevin. 1997. "EU Calls for Facilities for Pregnant Prisoners." *Irish Times* (Dublin), April 9.

Ó Tuathaigh, Gearóid. 1979. "The Role of Women in Ireland under the New English Order." In *Women in Irish Society: The Historical Dimension,* ed. Margaret MacCurtain and Donncha O'Corrain, 26–36. Contributions in Women's Studies no. 11. Westport: Greenwood Press.

POWs Maghaberry. 1992, "Monday 2nd March, 1992." In *Women in Struggle: Mina I Streachailt,* vol. 2, 4–5. Belfast: Sinn Fein Women's Department.

Quinn, Kathleen. 1993. "Silent Voices." *Theatre Ireland* 30 (winter): 9–11.

Roche, David. 1985. *Strip Searches at Her Majesty's Prison for Women, Armagh, Northern Ireland.* Gondregnies, Belgium: Irish Information Partnership.

Rockett, Kevin, et al. 1988. *Cinema and Ireland.* New York: Syracuse University Press.

———. 1994. "Culture, Industry, and Irish Cinema." In *Border Crossing: Film in Ireland, Britain, and Europe,* ed. John Hill et al., 126–39. Belfast: Institute of Irish Studies in association with the University of Ulster and the British Film Institute.

Rooney, Eilish. 1994. "Excluded Voices." *Fortnight: An Independent Review of Politics and the Arts* 322 (October): 28–29.

———. 1995a. "Political Division, Practical Alliance: Problems for Women in Conflict." *Journal of Women's History* 6, no. 4 and 7, no. 1 (winter–spring): 40–49.

———. 1995b. "Women in Political Conflict." *Race and Class* 1, no. 37: 51–55.

———. 1997. "Women in Party Politics and Local Groups: Findings from Belfast." In *Women in Irish Society: A Sociological Reader,* eds.

Anne Byrne and Madeleine Leonard. Belfast: Beyond the Pale Publications.

Roulston, Carmel. 1989. "Women on the Margin: The Women's Movement in Northern Ireland, 1973–1988." *Science & Society* 53, no. 2 (summer): 219–36.

Rubin, Gayle. 1970. "The Traffic in Women: Notes on the 'Political Economy' of Sex." In *Women, Class, and the Feminist Imagination: A Socialist-Feminist Reader,* ed. Karen V. Hansen and Ilene J. Philipson, 74–113. Philadelphia: Temple University Press.

Sinn Fein. 1992. "Women in Ireland." *Women's Policy Document.* Dublin and Belfast: Sinn Fein Head Office.

Smyth, Ailbhe. 1993. "The Women's Movement in the Republic of Ireland, 1970–1990," In *Irish Women's Studies Reader,* ed. Ailbhe Smyth, 245–67. Dublin: Attic Press.

———, ed. 1992. *The Abortion Papers.* Dublin: Attic Press.

Spivak, Gayatri. 1988a. *In Other Worlds: Essays in Cultural Politics.* New York: Routledge.

———. 1988b. "Can the Subaltern Speak?" In *Marxism and the Interpretation of Culture,* ed. Cary Nelson and Lawrence Grossberg, 271–313. Chicago: University of Illinois Press.

———. 1990. "The Politics of the Open End." In *The Post-Colonial Critic: Interviews, Strategies, Dialogues,* ed. Sarah Harasym, 95–112. New York: Routledge.

———. 1992. "Acting Bits/Identity Talk." *Critical Inquiry* 18, no. 4 (summer).

———. 1995a. "Ghostwriting." *Diacritics: A Review of Contemporary Criticism* 25, no. 2 (summer): 65–84.

———. 1995b. "Supplementing Marxism." In *Whither Marxism? Global Crisis in International Perspective,* ed. Bernd Magnus and Stephen Cullenberg, 109–19. New York and London: Routledge.

Sullivan, Megan. 1995. "Mary Beckett: An Interview." *Irish Literary Supplement* (spring): 10–12.

———. 1997. "*The Visit,* Incarceration, and Film by Women in Northern Ireland: An Interview with Orla Walsh." *Irish Review* 21 (autumn–winter): 29–40.

———. 1998. "From Nationalism to Baby X: An Interview with Margo Harkin." *Eire Ireland* (spring–summer): 40–51.

Tomlinson, Mike. 1980. *Northern Ireland: Between Civil Rights and Civil War,* ed. Liam O'Dowd, Bill Rolston, and Mike Tomlinson. London: CSE Books.

Trinh T. Minh-ha. 1991. *When the Moon Waxes Red: Representation, Gender, and Cultural Politics.* London and New York: Routledge.

"Twelve Months Later: Film Ireland Takes a Look Back at the Most Encouraging Year Ever for Irish Film." 1993–94. *Film Ireland* (December–January): 10.

Walsh, Orla, dir. 1992. *The Visit.* Film Base, Roisin Productions, Dublin.

Ward, Margaret, and Marie-Theresa McGivern. 1980. "Images of Women in Northern Ireland." *The Crane Bag* 4, no. 1: 579–85.

Warner, Marina. 1976. *Alone of All Her Sex: The Myth and the Cult of the Virgin Mary.* New York: Knopf.

White, Victoria. 1993. "Cathleen Ni Houlihan Is Not a Playwright." *Theatre Ireland* 30 (winter): 26–29.

Wilkins, Geraldine. 1994. "Film Production in Northern Ireland." In *Border Crossing: Film in Ireland, Britain, and Europe,* ed. John Hill et al., 126–39. Belfast: Institute of Irish Studies in association with the University of Ulster and the British Film Institute.

Williams, Caroline. 1993. "This Is One for the Sisters." *Theatre Ireland* 30 (winter): 6–8.

Wilmer, Steve. 1991. "Women's Theatre in Ireland." *New Theatre Quarterly* 7, no. 28 (November): 353–60.

# INDEX